Essential Jamaica

by

ANNIE WILSON

Annie Wilson is an experienced
travel writer and researcher
who has produced guides to holiday
destinations throughout the world.

AA

Produced by AA Publishing

Written by Annie Wilson
Peace and Quiet section
by Paul Sterry

Revised second edition
January1996
First published 1992

Edited, designed and produced by
AA Publishing.
© The Automobile Association 1996.
Maps © The Automobile Association
1996.

Distributed in the United Kingdom
by AA Publishing, Norfolk House,
Priestley Road, Basingstoke,
Hampshire, RG24 9NY.

A CIP catalogue record for this book
is available from the English Library.

ISBN 0 7495 1166 4

The Automobile Association retains
the copyright in the original edition
© 1992 and in all subsequent
editions, reprints and amendments
to editions listed above.

All rights reserved. No part of this
publication may be reproduced,
stored in a retrieval system, or
transmitted in any form or by any
means – electronic, photocopying,
recording or otherwise – unless the
written permission of the publishers
has been obtained beforehand. This
book may not be sold, resold, hired
out or otherwise disposed of by way
of trade in any form of binding or
cover other than that in which it is
published, without the prior consent
of the publisher.

The contents of this publication are
believed correct at the time of
printing. Nevertheless, the
publishers cannot be held
responsible for any errors or
omissions or for changes in the
details given in this guide or for the
consequences of any reliance on the
information provided by the same.
Assessments of attractions, hotels,
restaurants and so forth are based
upon the author's own experience
and, therefore, descriptions given in
this guide necessarily contain an
element of subjective opinion which
may not reflect the publisher's
opinion or dictate a reader's own
experience on another occasion.
**We have tried to ensure accuracy
in this guide, but things do change
and we would be grateful if
readers would advise us of any
inaccuracies they may encounter.**

Published by AA Publishing, a
trading name of Automobile
Association Developments Limited,
whose registered office is Norfolk
House, Priestley Road, Basingstoke,
Hampshire, RG24 9NY.
Registered number 1878835.

Colour separation: L C Repro,
Aldermaston

Printed by: Printers Trento, S.R.L.,
Italy

Front cover picture: Ocho Rios

Contents

This book employs a simple rating system to help choose which places to visit:

✓	'top ten'

◆◆◆ do not miss
◆◆ see if you can
◆ worth seeing if you have time

INTRODUCTION

A Caribbean island in the sun – the idyllic
images this conjures up are really there to be
found in Jamaica. And much more, if you take
the time to explore. Of course, there are the
seductive, soft white beaches, lapped by limpid
aquamarine seas and fringed by palms, where
you can bask in the sun. And the swish hotels
where the guests want for nothing. But these
are just part of the kaleidoscope of alternatives
that Jamaica can offer visitors. Jamaica's vibrant
character reflects its rich history, colourful
culture and natural beauty, which can make
your holiday a truly unique experience.
What strikes the eye first is the sumptuous
scenery. Jamaica is dominated by rugged
highlands, rising to the high, hazy peaks of the
Blue Mountains in the east. In places the slopes
plunge almost directly down to the coast; steep
valleys are cut by the clear waters of many
rivers, which spill over rocks in wonderful
waterfalls. The hillsides are smothered in
tropical forests, especially in the north, which is

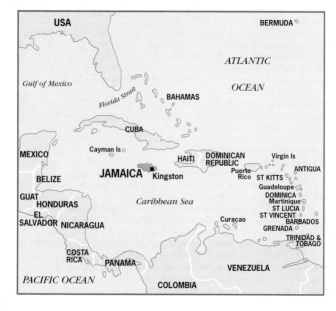

much greener than the south. Most visitors head for the north coast, and its sparkling strips of silvery sand hugged by hotels. This is where the busy, lively resorts and cruise ports of Montego Bay and Ocho Rios are. There is also the tranquil and much less touristy Port Antonio, set amid some of the island's loveliest scenery and beaches. On the west coast is Jamaica's most stunning beach, and the resort where everything and anything goes – Negril.

The south of the island has a very different atmosphere – it is relatively untouched by tourism as yet. Towards the east is the sprawling, noisy, dusty capital, Kingston, with its impressive harbour set against a beautiful backdrop of mountains. In the cool highlands inland is the genteel town of Mandeville. And the coast boasts quiet, secluded spots like the aptly-named Treasure Beach, and the quaint little town of Black River, backed by swampland which has a wealth of wildlife.

Jamaica aims to please, whether you're looking for *la dolce vita*, a merry-go-round of exciting activities, or an escapist's paradise where you can enjoy simple pleasures, absolute peace and nature at its best. It's a shame to stick to the popular spots on the north and west coast, or worse, to stay put in your hotel for two weeks. You may have a fabulous time, but this can give a rather slick, superficial view of Jamaica, and you miss out on its real and diverse character. It is possible to meet Jamaicans who can make your day, or even your whole holiday, a joy. They are justifiably proud of their beautiful island and they want you to enjoy it. So where is the hostility, the violence, and the crime that became associated with Jamaica some years ago? Visitors can rest easy about any rumours of Jamaica's dark heart – these were mostly the result of political tensions, inflamed during election times, and local disputes. As a visitor, you are unlikely to encounter any difficulties of this sort, or feel threatened, if you take care, as you would anywhere, and avoid the ghetto areas of Kingston (especially at night). Just show respect to the locals and their way of life – 'respect' is a much-used (and valued) word in Jamaica – and you will find them friendlier than people in many other parts of the world.

INTRODUCTION

Remember though, that Jamaica is a Third World country. Life isn't always easy for Jamaicans – although they seem so full of *joie de vivre* – and the island has known plenty of hardship in its turbulent and chequered past. Its heritage stems from a rich stew of different influences, including colonisation by the Spanish and then the British, both of whom imported slaves from Africa to work their plantations, and incursions by others (not least the buccaneers and pirates) who realised the attractions and strategic importance of the island.

As a result you will find people of every colour and ethnic origin – from African to Chinese, Indian, Jewish, Arabic and European. Their national independence motto is 'Out of many, one people'. The years of British rule have left an unmistakable legacy, from the educational and judiciary systems to cricket and driving on the left – there are also lots of familiar names, like Surrey, Middlesex and Cornwall, the three counties into which Jamaica is divided. But these names are mixed with others of Spanish and African origin. Even the language, though technically English, derives much from the melting pot of words, expressions and accents, so that the patois is practically incomprehensible to other English-speakers. This island has enchanted visitors for centuries – from Christopher Columbus to Noël Coward, Errol Flynn to Paul McCartney. The spectacularly beautiful scenery is enriched by the vivid flowers and scent of vanilla, spice or jasmine wafting in the breeze.

Your tastebuds will be sharpened by a tantalising array of local dishes, from piquant fresh fish to luscious fruits – and not forgetting the ubiquitous rum punches. And then, of course, there are the hypnotic rhythms of the music, especially reggae. Jamaica seduces the body and soul – but if you want to take your intellect off the back-burner, it is well worth delving into the history, culture and legends of the island. Problems are forgotten here, and everything 'soon come' to those who relax into the laid-back rhythm of life. Then, without question, you will believe everything is 'irie', as they say in Jamaica.

BACKGROUND

Geography

Jamaica's landscapes are the stage on which its dramatic character unfolds.

It is the third largest island in the Caribbean, sitting 28 degrees north of the equator, 90 miles (145km) south of Cuba. Said to be shaped like a swimming turtle, Jamaica is about 145 miles (233km) long from Negril to Morant Point, and 50 miles (80km) at its widest point (north to south). A central backbone of mountains stretches from the west, along the curious pitted plateau of Cockpit Country, to the ethereal eastern peaks of the Blue Mountains. They reach heavenward through the clouds, rising to 7,402 feet (2,256m) only 10 miles (16km) from the coastal plain near Kingston. More than half the island lies 1,000 feet (300m) above the sparkling turquoise seas that surround it. In places it is honeycombed with impressive cave systems that show the oceanic origins of this landscape, which was thrust up from the sea-bed by volcanic activity millions of years ago.

Although it is the sunshine that epitomises the warm character of the island, rainfall on the mountains and northern coast results in distinctive differences in the scenery. The highlands and slopes rising from the north coast are generally luxuriantly wooded; while the wider coastal plains along the south look much drier, with landscapes like the African savannah or Mediterranean scrub in many places.

Trees and bush vegetation proliferate all over Jamaica, even in the drier areas, but there are also many areas of grassy fields and plantations where the woods were cleared by Europeans in past centuries. Here cattle graze, or stand quietly in the cool shade of palm and mango trees, always accompanied by white egrets (a heron-like bird) which eat their ticks.

There are more than 120 rivers on the island, which tumble down through mountain gorges to the coastal plains and sea, swelled to raging torrents by high rains or reduced to boulder-strewn gullies in dry weather.

The island's beautiful beaches are a prime tourist attraction. Many nestle in coves, bordered by rocks and cliffs, and are protected

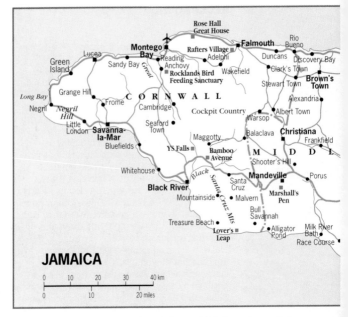

JAMAICA

by coral reefs from which the pale sands have been formed (as well as the offshore cays and islets).

Towns and villages tend to be scruffy, haphazard settlements. And the sophisticated hotels along the north coast are in stark contrast to the simple, shabby clapboard or breeze-block homes with corrugated zinc roofs in which most Jamaicans live. The tourist development along the north coast is not continuous; although it spreads out from the resorts (especially Montego Bay, Ocho Rios and the area between them), there are stretches that are quite unspoilt. But you do see touches of tourism that are missing from the south coast – such as numerous craft stalls beside the road, signs for rooms to rent or restaurants, and simply more foreign white faces. For a truly unspoilt taste of Jamaica, you must explore inland or the south.

However, from the north coast, you need only go a few miles inland and into the hills to find complete peace and superb panoramas –

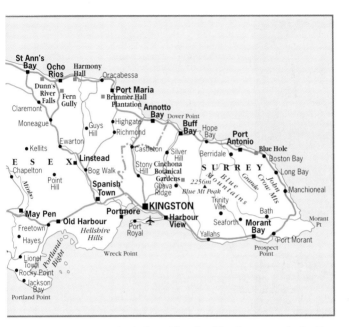

typical rural Jamaica. The slopes are cloaked in a confusion of jungly foliage; the tall trees adorned with tangles of trailing creepers and vines, and the dark green spangled with the sizzling scarlet blooms of the flame of the forest of poinciana trees. Along the roads are scattered brightly-painted shacks, and groups of locals sit gossiping and laughing outside open bar-shops while goats wander around nibbling the shrubs. Small patches of yams, sweet peppers or citrus trees are cultivated around the houses; donkeys, heavily-laden with crops like sticks of sugar cane, vie with battered buses packed to the roof-racks; there is often a boy carrying a bucket of water on his head or a man with a precariously-balanced pile of bananas and breadfruit; women sell exotic fruit like paw-paw or ackee by the roadside, or wash clothes in the river and lay them out to dry on the hot rocks; a dreadlocked woolly-hatted Rasta may be glimpsed smoking *ganja*. And as you pass by, cute kids in school uniforms shout cheeky greetings. Most of life

BACKGROUND

takes place outside in Jamaica.

Sugar cane, bananas, coffee and citrus fruit were introduced by the Spanish colonists and became important export crops. Sugar is still a major crop, and you will see big plantations with acres of long spear-like cane leaves waving in the breeze; sugar is also distilled into various types of famous Jamaica rum. The emerald-green banana palms can be seen growing everywhere in people's backyards, but the most extensive plantations are along the northeast coast. Coffee is grown in the mountains, and Blue Mountain coffee is world-renowned. The inland highland areas around Mandeville are well-known for citrus fruit of many types. Other cash crops include tobacco, coconuts, cocoa, pimento (a tree producing allspice – the only one of these that is a native of Jamaica), and *ganja* (marijuana, first introduced by workers from India) which, of course, is illegal.

Jamaica is one of the world's main bauxite producers, and this is vital to the island's economy, being one of its biggest export earners. However, the industry on which Jamaica relies most heavily is tourism. As such an important source of foreign exchange, in the light of the serious economic (and political) problems they have had to face, it is not surprising the government has worked hard to promote a positive image of late. Very many of the island's inhabitants are directly or indirectly employed by tourism, and they want to ensure Jamaica remains attractive to visitors – whose money provides opportunities where there might be none in a country of high unemployment and poverty.

History
First Settlers

Jamaica's original inhabitants were Arawak Indians, who first arrived from South America in about AD650. Until the Spanish colonists settled here centuries later, the Arawaks thrived on the island they called *Xaymaca* (meaning 'land of wood and water'). These Indians were a peaceful people who were skilled artisans, but all that remains of the Arawak culture are various artefacts and cave paintings found near

Left: wood carvings

village sites – and a few words like 'hammock' (which they invented, and wove from the cotton they grew), 'canoe', 'tobacco', 'barbecue' and 'hurricane'.

It was in 1494 that Christopher Columbus arrived at Jamaica, landing on the north coast and claiming the island in the name of the Spanish crown. He said it was the 'fairest island that eyes have beheld'. The Spanish colonists began arriving around 1510, and established their first settlement of Sevilla la Nueva (New Seville) near St Ann's Bay in the north. But 25 years later they abandoned it for a more propitious site in the south: Villa de la Vega was the new capital, eventually to be simply called Spanish Town. Lying west of Kingston, it remained Jamaica's capital until 1872.

The island became a backwater of the Spanish colonies. There was no gold, as had been hoped, and it was used principally as a base to supply Spanish ships. But they did introduce some important crops, including sugar cane and bananas. The Spanish destroyed the native Arawak population: they were forced into hard labour, cruelly mistreated and also affected by European diseases to which they had no immunity. In 1517, the Spanish started importing slaves from Africa to replace the Arawaks. But under Spanish rule, Jamaica suffered increasingly from neglect, internal strife, and raids by pirates and European forces jealous of Spain's powerful grip on the Caribbean.

Enter the English

A large expeditionary fleet, sent from England by Oliver Cromwell, was defeated in an attack on Hispaniola (now Haiti and the Dominican Republic) – so they decided to go on to the weaker island of Jamaica. In 1655, the English sailed into what is now Kingston Harbour and marched to Spanish Town. But the Spaniards had fled to the north coast and on to Cuba – taking with them their valuables and freeing their slaves.

The retreating Spanish left arms with their slaves, instructing them to harass the invaders until they had an opportunity to return. The slaves took to the most inaccessible highlands and from these wild areas made surprise attacks on the British for over a century. These people became known as the Maroons (from the Spanish *cimarrón*, meaning 'wild' or 'living on peaks').

A Spanish attempt at recapturing Jamaica failed after a fierce battle at Rio Nuevo, on the north coast, in 1658. Finally, the island was ceded to the English crown under the Treaty of Madrid (1670). There is little evidence today of this period of Spanish rule – except various names.

Pirates and Privateers

Under the British, Jamaica saw increasing prosperity – despite tempestuous times – and became one of the most valuable colonies of the Caribbean. In the early days, the buccaneers brought riches to the island. They had originally been a motley crew of renegades who hunted pigs and cattle in the north of Hispaniola, and traded with passing ships. Their name comes from *boucan*, the wooden frame on which they cured the meat. The buccaneers banded together, and with captured Spanish ships and arms, began making raids further afield – and plundered more glittering prizes than pork. Some of their terrorist activities were made legal by letters of marque, issued by the English and French to encourage harassment of the Spanish by privateers. Port Royal (by Kingston Harbour) became the buccaneers' home base, where they traded and spent their booty – carousing and debauchery were the order of the day (and night). Their lair became known as 'the richest, and wickedest, city in the world'. Henry Morgan, a ruthless and resourceful Welshman, was a renowned leader among the 'Brethren of the Coast'. After a rumbustious buccaneering career, he was tried for piracy in London, aquitted on patriotic grounds and then knighted. He returned to Jamaica to become governor – and, with amazing audacity, tried to crack down on buccaneering! When he died in 1688, he was buried with state honours in his beloved Port Royal.

The demise of this buccaneering capital came four years later, when it was toppled into the sea by an earthquake. Throughout the 18th

century there was conflict in the Caribbean between the British, Spanish and French, and pirates continued to plague ships and coastal areas. Among these colourful characters was 'Calico Jack' Rackham, who liked to wear calico underwear; after being captured in Negril Harbour, two of his toughest crew members were found to be women. (Anne Bonney, who escaped punishment as she was pregnant, and Mary Read). As protection against such incursions, the British built many forts. Port Royal became an important naval station, and it was here at Fort Charles that a young Horatio Nelson was given a command post in 1779.

Maroons in the Mountains

In the late 17th and early 18th centuries, the British were also beset by internal attacks from the Maroons. Concentrated in the remote areas of Cockpit Country and the northeastern mountains (where their descendants still live today), they remained fiercely independent and continued to beleaguer the British empire-builders. They swept down from the hills at night to set fire to fields and steal stock. Their numbers were swelled by Breakaways, slaves who escaped the plantations. In 1690, forces of rebel slaves, led by a general called Cudjoe, joined with the Maroons to launch the First Maroon War (the Second War was in 1795). Skilled at using the forests and caves of their rugged home terrain to avoid capture by the better-armed troops – and using ingenious methods of ambush, disguising themselves with branches and leaves – the Maroons fought a hard guerilla war. The Windward Maroons in the Blue Mountains were led by the indomitable and courageous warrior priestess, Queen Nanny – reputed to repel enemy fire with her backside! Although Nanny Town was destroyed, the Maroons were never conquered. But finally, the Cockpit Maroons agreed peace terms in 1739, and the Blue Mountain Maroons the following year. This treaty guaranteed them a considerable measure of self-government, which they still enjoy today. And the 'Right Excellent Nanny' and Cudjoe have entered the realms of national legend.

Slaves and Sugar

Jamaica's sugar plantations grew and multiplied – along with the slave trade. The huge sugar estates reached their heyday in the 18th century – the island had 57 in 1673, which leapt to 430 by 1739 – bringing great prosperity and power to their owners. Rich planters built elegant Great Houses and enjoyed a life of lavish luxury (often in Europe), while their slaves lived a miserable existence of forced labour and brutal subjugation. By 1800 there were 300,000 slaves, 15 times the number of whites on the island.

The slaves were ruled with a rod of iron, since their despised white masters constantly feared uprisings in which they might be murdered or the plantation destroyed. In 1760, a slave called Tacky led a serious revolt in the Port Maria area on the north coast; and Tacky's Rebellion sparked off uprisings in other areas. After several months of terrible bloodshed, the revolts were stamped out.

Political reforms in Britain led to the abolition of the slave trade in 1807. But Jamaica's ruling class fiercely opposed the emancipation of slaves – and the Nonconformist missionaries who supported the slaves' cause. The unrest culminated in another bloody rebellion in 1831, instigated by 'Daddy' Sam Sharpe, a Baptist preacher; the square in Montego Bay where he was hanged now bears his name. It signalled the end of slavery, and full emancipation was granted by the British Parliament in 1838. However, having left the estates, the freed slaves lived in abject poverty with no means of improving their conditions. Baptist preacher Paul Bogle led a protest that became the Morant Bay Rebellion, in 1865. It was put down with great severity – more than 400 protesters were shot or hanged (including Bogle), hundreds flogged and thousands of homes destroyed. Sam Sharpe and Paul Bogle have both become national heroes.

Many of the Great Houses were burnt during the slave rebellions. And after the abolition of slavery, the plantations and sugar production fell into decline – despite efforts to bring in workers from elsewhere. But at the end of the 19th century, bananas began to boom.

Left: the 1865
rebellion

Independence

Under the new Crown Colony system of
government, Jamaica saw some reforms and
improvements by the turn of the century, but it
was hit hard by the depression in the 1930s.
Discontent grew due to many factors – growing
unemployment, economic difficulties such as
the devastation of the banana industry through
disease, the fact that most blacks still had no
vote – and finally erupted in widespread rioting
and violence in 1938. Two important figures
emerged at this time: Alexander Bustamante, a
Trade Unionist who later formed the Labour
Party; and Norman Manley, a leading barrister
who founded the People's National Party. Their
campaigns for better wages and working
conditions, along with political reform, paved
the way for the new constitution of 1944, based
on universal adult suffrage. Complete political
independence for Jamaica came on 6 August
1962 – as a self-governing member of the
British Commonwealth.

Since then, Jamaica has maintained a strong
democratic spirit, although politics arouse
volatile and stormy passions.

The People

Jamaica has about two and a half million
inhabitants. A third of them live in Kingston, while
60 per cent live in rural areas. The vast majority
are black, descendants of the slaves shipped
over from many different tribes in Africa. Up to
1838, Britain and Africa had been the ancestral
countries of nearly all the island's inhabitants –
apart from a few Spanish and Portuguese Jews.
Then after the abolition of slavery, workers and
servants were recruited from India, China, even
Germany, Scotland and Ireland; Syrians (from
what is now Lebanon) arrived as salesmen.
Their descendants have added to the ethnic mix
today, in which the percentage of white
Jamaicans is very small. But these minority
groups have influence that far outweighs their
numbers; and most of the wealthy people in
Jamaica are white. Mixed marriage has resulted
in the exciting range of skin tones and facial
features to be seen in Jamaica. But, although 'Out
of many, one people' have been created, they
still live in a stratified society.

BACKGROUND

Slavery has had an indelible effect on Jamaica's heritage – apart from bringing in the majority race. For example, slaves were encouraged to have children but not allowed long-term relationships, and this is still reflected in the pattern of family life today. Many women have several children before (if ever) getting married, and the children are looked after by female members of the family – who are characteristically strong and independent. (But that is not to say that men don't have very sexist attitudes to women.) Under British rule, the mulattos were given more favours and power than their black half-brothers, creating a hierarchy that still survives.

Religion has always played an important role here – perhaps as a source of hope in a hard life – from the Catholic priests who wanted to save the souls of the Arawaks and Africans, to the uniquely Jamaican Rastafarians. As with other aspects of Jamaican culture that have combined different ethnic influences, Christianity has been blended with African beliefs and rituals. Cults still practised by a few – or which have contributed elements to Afro-Christian sects – include *Obeah* and *Myal* (sorcery), and related cults *Kumina* (meaning to move with rhythm) and *Bongo*, which believe in the power of *duppies* (ghosts), and use drumming, dancing and spiritual trances. The Baptist missionaries were important in the abolitionist movement at the beginning of the 19th century and so Nonconformist religions have had more success in introducing Christian practices. African beliefs merged with the Baptist faith at that time to produce the Revival movement, with sects like *Pocomania*. Now the most popular denominations are Anglican, Baptist and Methodist – but there is a variety of other faiths and sects to be found. American-style fundamentalists have grown in popularity in recent years, with plenty of singing and hand-clapping.

Rastafarianism has had a profound effect on Jamaican society, both on the island and abroad. It was founded by Marcus Garvey, who set up the Universal Negro Improvement Association in 1914, awakening black consciousness and pride, and advocating the

Right: jerk pork and coconut water

'back to Africa' cause. When Ras Tafari was crowned Emperor of Ethiopia, taking the name Haile Selassie ('Might of the Trinity'), he was regarded as the Black Messiah. And Ethiopia was the promised land to which the lost black tribe of Israel would one day return. In the depressed 1930s, the poor folk of Jamaica were ready for a new religion of hope. Its adherents live according to a code which includes living in harmony with nature and *Jah* (God), believing everyone is equal, opposing greed and exploitation, desiring no more than the essentials of life, not eating meat and shellfish (or drinking alcohol), Bible reading and smoking the sacramental herb *ganja*.

Rastas do not cut their hair, and their distinctive dreadlocks are inspired by the sacred symbol of the lion (taken from one of Selassie's titles, Lion of Judah), as well as African hairstyles. Some of their beliefs may seem confusing and illogical (this applies to most religions), but true Rastas are peaceful, honest, spiritual people. And out of their non-violent protest against oppression grew reggae. The development of this universally popular Jamaican music has been inextricably linked with Rastafarianism – and has produced many stars, notably Bob Marley and the Wailers. Some of the trappings of the Rasta movement – especially the hairstyle – have been taken up by people jumping on the bandwagon. The red, green and gold colours, which you see everywhere, come from the Ethiopian flag. Many words that are part of the dialect developed by Rastas have been assimilated into common Jamaican patois. Rastafarianism has given many Jamaicans an identity of their own and a pride in their nationality, and in being black.

Music – along with singing and dancing – has always been close to the heart of Jamaicans. Its roots lie in the African traditions the slaves brought with them. Other musical influences were absorbed to produce sounds uniquely Jamaican. First came *mento*, descended from a sensuous dance the slaves created combining African and European elements. Slow and rhythmic with saucy lyrics, *mento* remained strong until the 1950s (not to be confused with calypso, from Trinidad). The influence of

BACKGROUND

American rhythm-and-blues gave rise, in the 1960s, to the funky beat of ska and the more languid rock-steady, which achieved universal popularity. The heavy bass rhythms of reggae, often with words of protest, were born in the late 1960s. It soon made an international impact, creating a booming music industry in Jamaica. Reggae remains ever-popular, and continues to evolve – in turn influencing other music. Jamaican rap has developed with the thriving 'dancehall' scene, where the music is loud and the pace is racy.

Artistic talent blooms in Jamaica. The love of colour and drama can be seen reflected in everyday life; a simple bar will have bright designs painted on the walls, while a game of dominoes can be a performance art.

Jamaica has real cultural treats for those who look further afield than the native folk shows put on for tourists, such as Kingston's National Gallery of Art, the National Dance Theatre Company, and National Pantomine.

Jamaicans are a proud people. Those you meet – especially in rural areas – are generally welcoming, open and extremely down-to-earth.

However, since visitors seem so well-off compared to most locals (and they certainly see it that way), you will be expected to spend money freely and hand out tips at the slightest opportunity. This is particularly so in touristy places, where the persistent hassling to buy things can be a problem. It's mainly a symptom of the contrast between rich and poor, and much less likely to be encountered in the southern or inland areas which have not yet been affected by a proliferation of smart hotels and tourists.

If you are interested in really understanding the Jamaican way of life and meeting the locals, find out about the Jamaica Tourist Board's 'Meet The People' scheme. Or contact Diana McIntyre-Pike, at the Astra Country Inn in Mandeville, who energetically promotes 'community tourism' and Country-style holidays (especially around the south, but she is a fount of useful advice about all Jamaica – see page 93). It could help you make the most of your visit.

NORTHWEST AND WEST

Doctor's Cave Beach, Montego Bay

Lying in the county of Cornwall, this area covers the parishes of St James, Trelawny, Hanover and the northern parts of Westmoreland. It boasts two of the island's three main resorts, namely Montego Bay and Negril, where most of Jamaica's visitors stay (along with Ocho Rios, see page 38). Hotels spread along the coast either side of Montego Bay, behind pretty sandy beaches. A variety of amenities aimed at tourists are scattered beside the busy main road heading east, including bar shacks and souvenir stands. But parts of the coast are quite unspoilt, especially in Hanover. There are pastures, dotted with trees and grazing cattle, and fields of tall, rustling sugar cane along the narrow coastal plain, which has a backdrop of wooded hills and valleys. Inland the scenery becomes much more dramatic – and the tempo more peaceful. The jungly hillsides around Montego Bay climb to 1,850 feet (564m) just a few miles inland. To the southeast are the mysterious highlands of Cockpit Country. Hanover, to the west, is also mountainous inland, with a rocky coastline. Some of its bays and coves have strips of silvery sand, but the beaches are less good as you put Montego Bay behind you – the rocks and coral reefs in shallow seas make bathing difficult. The best beach is on the western tip of the island at Negril: miles of shimmering sand and turquoise sea, with the resort lying beside it.

Relax on Negril's idyllic beach

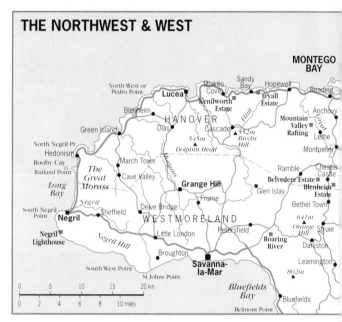

THE NORTHWEST & WEST

MONTEGO BAY

North West or Pedro Point • **Lucea** • Mishito Cove • Sandy Bay • Hopewell • Reading

Kenilworth Estate • Tryall Estate

Blenheim • Dias • H A N O V E R • Cascade • 552m Birchs Hill • Mountain Valley Rafting • Lethe • Anchovy

Green Island • 515m • Dolphin Head • Montpelier

North Negril Pt • Hedonism • March Town • Ramble • Chester Castle

Booby Cay • Rutland Point • *The Great Morass* • Cave Valley • **Grange Hill** • Belvedere Estate • Glen Islay • Blenheim Estate

Long Bay • *Negril* • Frome • Bethel Town

South Negril Point • **Negril** • Delve Bridge • W E S T M O R E L A N D • 641m Orange Hill • Struie

Negril Lighthouse • Sheffield • Little London • Petersfield • Roaring River • Daniston

Negril Hill • Broughton • Leamington

South West Point • St Johns Point • **Savanna-la-Mar** • 802m

| 0 | 5 | 10 | 15 | 20 km |
| 0 | 2 | 4 | 6 | 8 | 10 miles |

Bluefields Bay • Bluefields

Belmont Point

WHAT TO SEE

MONTEGO BAY

MoBay, as it is nicknamed, is
Jamaica's second 'city' (after
Kingston). It sprawls up slopes
behind the fine bay. Described
as 'the gulf of good weather' by
Columbus, in the Spanish era it
was used for shipping pig lard,
manteca, from which its name
probably originates. Then it
became an important sugar and
banana port. Now life revolves
around its major industry:
tourism. It is Jamaica's tourist
capital, and one of the most
popular resorts in the Caribbean.
Here there are top-notch hotels
and sports galore – but not much
authentic Jamaican atmosphere,
except in the down-beat
downtown backstreets.

At the heart of MoBay is **Sam
Sharpe Square**. In one corner is
the **Cage**, once used to
imprison errant slaves. Beside it
is a statue of Sam Sharpe, the
preacher who led the 1831
slave rebellion – and was
hanged here. The area around
the Square, with its narrow
streets, is a hive of activity
where the noise of the traffic
competes with vendors touting
wares such as T-shirts and fruit.
Some of the Georgian houses
nearby have been restored,
including two fine merchants'
houses which are now
restaurants: **The Georgian
House** (on the corner of Union
and Orange Streets), and the

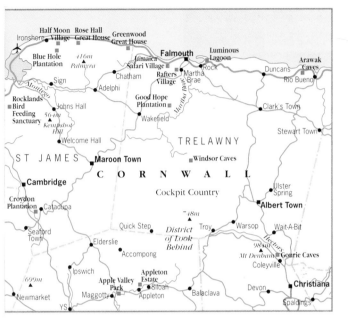

Town House (on Church Street – see page 25). Opposite stands **St James Parish Church**, dating from 1775 (and rebuilt after the 1957 earthquake); it is also well worth a look as a reflection of a bygone age of elegance.

Towards the waterfront lies the main **Crafts Market**, a lively spot where tourists barter for souvenirs. Boat trips leave from Pier One, beside the busy harbour nearby. The remains of **Fort Montego** sit on a slope north of here, by Walter Fletcher Beach, with two cannons pointing out to sea – next to it is another Crafts Market. Heading north, Gloucester Avenue hugs the shoreline; with its hotels, restaurants, shops and beach, it

hums with tourist activity day and night. Roads climb the hill behind, to the airport on the coast north of town. South of the centre, off Barnett Street, is the **Fustic Road Market** – full of hustle and bustle in real Jamaican style, especially on Fridays and Saturdays.

A very different world is to be found at **Montego Bay Freeport**, southwest of here. This is the location of the cruise ship wharf, the ultra-smart Montego Bay Yacht Club, and a large duty-free shopping centre. There are three main town beaches, with fine white sand and sheltered swimming. They charge a small entrance fee and have a variety of facilities, from changing rooms to sports.

Jah David, a Crafts Marketeer

roads behind the public beaches. The large and more up-market hotels lie along the coastal strip either side of the resort, behind private beaches. Two of the top hotels are set several miles west of MoBay, with plush rooms and villas in beautiful estates by the sea – where very high prices will provide the class, sophistication and facilities to match. Secluded on a lush peninsula, **Round Hill** (tel: 952 5150) is a truly charming hotel; tastefully designed in plantation-house and ethnic styles, it has an exclusive understated elegance. A few miles further west lies **Tryall Golf, Tennis and Beach Club** (tel: 956 5660), whose main buildings are in an 18th-century Great House, sparkling white and beautifully furnished; it sits on a hillside overlooking the coast and its grounds (including its famous golf course).

Two other classy hotels lie on the coast east of MoBay. The swish **Half Moon Golf, Tennis and Beach Club** (tel: 953 2211) is eminently elegant and sophisticated, with luxurious suites and many sumptuous villas set in extensive tropical gardens; it has recently added a fine Equestrian Centre to its excellent range of facilities. Nearby is the rather less expensive **Coyaba Beach Club** (tel: 953 9150). This is an intimate hotel with spacious suites and tasteful décor; it has an exclusive, personal atmosphere and much charm. Also on the coast to the east is

Walter Fletcher Beach lies nearest the centre. MoBay's attractive **Doctor's Cave Beach**, by Gloucester Avenue, has been popular since the 1920s; it gained renown after a doctor claimed its waters had healing powers. **Cornwall Beach**, up the road, is smaller but also popular; behind it is the Tourist Board office and a crafts complex. Just north of here is **Sunset Lodge Beach**, where you can bathe free.

Accommodation

MoBay offers a very wide choice of accommodation, from some of the smartest hotels in the Caribbean to simple guest houses. Most of the more moderately-priced places are in town, particularly along the

the large, efficient, American-style, high-rise **Wyndham Rose Hall Beach Hotel** (tel: 953 2650), which has its own golf course. Closer to MoBay is **Sandals Royal Jamaican** (tel: 953 2231), and near the airport its sister hotel, **Sandals Montego Bay** (tel: 952 5510); these are all-inclusive resort hotels for couples only, where everything from a wealth of sports and activities to drinks and tips is included in the price.

On the hotel strip behind the beaches to the north of town is the smaller, cheaper **Sandals Inn** (tel: 952 4140), whose guests can use facilities at the other Sandals hotels. Just along the road lies the moderately-priced **Doctor's Cave Beach Hotel** (tel: 952 4355) and slightly lower-priced **Fantasy Resort** (tel: 952 4150); both are comfortable, with good facilities including a pool. An alternative with a great deal of character is the small **Richmond Hill Inn** (tel: 952 3859), in an 18th-century Great House perched on a quiet hill above the town with superb views (and a pool);

it has a smart, old-fashioned style.

For the budget-conscious, the **Toby Inn** (tel: 952 4370) is a neat, friendly hotel next to the Fantasy, with a pool set in gardens. And towards the airport, **La Mirage** (tel: 952 4435) is a modern little hotel, with a pool and great views. The neighbouring **Chatwick Gardens** (tel: 952 2147) charges even lower rates; it also has a pool. Nearby are the **Seville Guest House and Villas** (tel: 952 2814), with a pool, and homely **Ocean View Guest House** (tel: 952 2662).

East of Falmouth is the large **Trelawny Beach Hotel** (tel: 954 2450), which also has cottage units set in gardens; the all-inclusive prices are reasonable, and activities abound, including a special range for children. Several miles south of Falmouth, in beautiful rolling countryside by the Martha Brae River, is **Good Hope** (tel: 954 3289), a splendid Great House dating from 1744

The world-class Tryall Golf Club

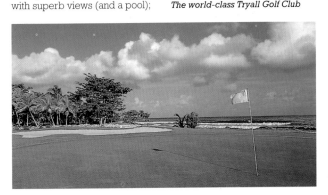

which is now a small, personal, higher-priced hotel; enchantingly tranquil and stylish, it is surrounded by gardens (with a pool) and a working plantation which can be explored on horse-back.

Nightlife and Entertainment

There is no lack of choice if you are looking for organised trips – full details can be obtained from your hotel or local Tourist Board office. One of the most popular is the **Appleton Express**, a jolly trip that travels through some splendid inland countryside. En route it stops at Catadupa, a village on the edge of Cockpit Country, and then continues southeast to the Appleton Rum Distillery for a guided tour and lunch; it also stops for a visit to the Ipswich Caves (see page 33).

The **Hilton High Day Tour** passes through beautiful mountain countryside inland for Jamaican breakfast and lunch at the Hilton Plantation House, where you can tour the estate, go up in a hot-air balloon, walk to Seaford Town (see page 37), or go horse-riding.

Organised trips are available to many of the sights listed in **What Else To See In The Northwest** (see page 32), and other areas of the island.

There are many different boat cruises offered. These trips often include drinks, lunch, snorkelling, or visits along the coast, such as to Miskito Cove for a picnic, or to Negril; there are also sunset cruises or night-time glass-bottomed boat trips. A popular night-time excursion is an **Evening on the Great River** (west of MoBay), with a ride in a fishing canoe up the torch-lit river, then a stop for a Jamaican barbecue, a folklore show and dancing to live music. There is also lots of fun to be had at one of MoBay's weekly **Beach Parties**, which include dinner, entertainment and an evening of reggae under the stars. MoBay offers a variety of action after dark. The major hotels have nightly entertainment; and there are also discos, for example, at the **Seawind Beach Resort**, **Fantasy Resort**, **Holiday Inn** and **Trelawny Beach Hotel**. A hot pace is set at the Friday-night disco at **Pier 1 On The Waterfront** (a restaurant on Howard Cooke Boulevard). Reggae fans should try **Sir Winston's** (Gloucester Avenue). On Monday evenings Gloucester Avenue is closed to cars for the **MoBay Nite Out**, a carnival of live music, dance and shows, plus an array of local food and art to enjoy.

The Jamaica Carnival takes place in April; and in August you can hear reggae galore at the **Reggae Summerfest**, held at the Bob Marley Performing Centre (contact the Tourist Board for details and dates).

Restaurants

There are plenty of restaurants, from those in swank hotels to basic snack bars and stalls, from US-style fast food to Chinese. Many restaurants offer free transport to and from hotels. Several of the hotels have good restaurants – including the **Richmond Hill Inn** (tel: 952 3859), with a romantic view of the twinkling lights of MoBay from its open-air terrace. There is also the **Sugar Mill** restaurant at the Half Moon Club (tel: 953 2314), which is highly regarded. The **Town House**, Church Street (tel: 952 2660) is one of the best-known restaurants, lying near the centre in an 18th-century merchant's house with a pretty flowery courtyard; it has a menu of delicious fresh fish and Jamaican or American-style dishes – tasty food in an attractive ambience.

Marguerite's By The Sea, Gloucester Avenue (tel: 952 4777), is a pretty place with a terrace right on the sea, overlooking the bay – and it serves good fish.

West of MoBay, by the harbour at Reading, is **Norma's Wharf House** (tel: 952 2745), in a restored old sugar mill on the waterfront; it offers classy gourmet dishes.

Shopping

MoBay has lots of opportunities for shopping. Generally items are cheaper in downtown shops than along the tourist strip, or at hotel shops out of town. There are plenty of modern shopping plazas – with duty-free shops selling watches, jewellery, cameras, electrical goods, crystal, china and perfume – such as the **City Centre Building** and **Life of Jamaica Shopping Centre** near the centre of town, **St James Place Shopping Arcade** by Cornwall Beach, and **Montego Bay Freeport Shopping Centre**. Other places include the **Overton Shopping Plaza** up the

Music on the streets, Montego Bay

hill on Union Street, the **Beachview Shopping Plaza** on Gloucester Avenue, plus the **Blue Diamond** and **Holiday Village Shopping Centres** by Ironshore (east of MoBay). The two **Crafts Markets** (on Harbour Street and by Fort Montego) are the places to go to bargain for locally-made straw hats, baskets and mats, wooden carvings, T-shirts, tie-dyed clothes and shell jewellery. Good quality Jamaican paintings and carvings can be found at the **Gallery of West Indian Art** at 1 Orange Lane, or the **Bay Gallery** on Gloucester Avenue. For an extravaganza of everyday goods, including food, visit the **Fustic Street Market**.

Sports

No problem, here, either – whatever you enjoy. Your hotel or the Tourist Board will provide up-to-the-minute information.

There are excellent opportunities for watersports of every kind. The **Montego Bay Marine Park**, for example, has a huge area of magical coral reefs for divers to explore. Golfers can choose between four championship courses (**Tryall**, **Half Moon**, **Wyndham Rose Hall** and **Ironshore**). Several places offer horse-riding, such as the fine new **Equestrian Centre** at the Half Moon Club, and the **Good Hope Plantation** which has miles of marked trails.

◆◆◆
NEGRIL

This place was originally named Negrillo by the Spanish. Its harbour occasionally sheltered the English fleet and pirates in the 18th century. Until 30 years

Guiding light: Negril lighthouse

ago, Negril was no more than a small, isolated fishing village, without phones or electricity. Then it became an escapists' haven for Rastas and itinerant hippies, who lived the natural life in huts and tents along the beach. Word got around about its unspoilt beauty, and in the early 1980s the explosion of tourist development started. Negril's major attraction is its superb, seven-mile (11km) stretch of luminous white sands. The resort hugs the coastline, running either side of the road the whole length of the beach and along the cliffs to the south. It is very different to Montego Bay and Ocho Rios in that it has not developed around a town; it is purely a resort and feels as if it has no life of its own apart from tourism. Despite the commercialisation, it is an appealing resort – no buildings rise higher than the palm trees and many are designed in attractive 'ethnic' styles, surrounded by gardens. Negril has a light-hearted, colourful atmosphere, with the emphasis on relaxation and pleasures. More than anywhere else on the island, you can do as you please here – including sunbathe nude or party all night. The centre of Negril lies at the junction of the beach road and the cliff-top road, where the road from the south coast enters the resort. Near the roundabout is a central square with shopping complexes (including the Tourist Board office), and the **Negril Craft Park** which is set behind the beach. Here also, the South Negril River runs into the sea; boats are moored along it, and nearby are jetties from which various boat trips leave. The northern section of the resort lies along Norman Manley Boulevard, behind Long Bay, up to **Bloody Bay** (Negril Harbour) in the north. This bay, with its pretty crescent of sand, was a less peaceful spot in the past. It is where the infamous pirate 'Calico Jack' Rackham was captured; but its name dates from the days when whalers cleaned their catch here. Bloody Bay is divided from Long Bay by Rutland Point, and offshore you can see **Booby Cay**, a coral islet which can be visited by boat. Negril's airstrip and the Rutland Point Craft Market are set inland of the coast road here.

Long Bay is the pride of Negril: miles of dazzling-white soft sand bathed in the translucent, aquamarine sea, which is calm and perfect for swimming, protected by a coral reef further out. A beachcomber's delight – the beach is so long it does not feel crowded, although there is plenty of action here. Upper parts of the beach in front of hotels are often private, with beach beds, bars, palm-thatched shelters and hammocks. Masses of watersports and excursions are available, from waterskiing to parasailing, snorkelling, diving, glass-bottomed boat trips and windsurfing. There are also lots of locals selling souvenirs. The most peaceful parts of the beach are towards the north. Inland of the beach road is a flat landscape of low bush and swamp – the **Great Morass**. These peaty wetlands are an

area of National Park, where many interesting birds and plants may be found.
The southern section of Negril lies along the narrow, winding West End Road which skirts the cliffs and rocky coves around to **Negril Lighthouse**. There are good views from the top of this 100-foot (30m) landmark, which has guided sailors round the coast for 100 years. Some of the cheaper accommodation lies along here, including palm-thatched huts perched on the cliff-tops. It is the most easy-going end of the resort, with little sophistication, but lots of life. The sunsets are seen at their best from this southwesterly point, and **Rick's Café** is the most popular spot to catch this spectacular natural show, as well as watch daring young divers plunge into the waves from the cliffs.
Since Negril is one long development that sticks to the beach and cliffs, you can quickly leave the resort behind to explore the quiet surrounding countryside. The land rises east of West End Road, up the slopes of **Negril Hill**; there are splendid views from the old plantation estate of Whitehall, visited on horse-riding tours.

Accommodation

Almost all the accommodation is spread along the coast. The larger, more up-market hotels are towards the north end of Long Bay, while the cheaper (and often more characterful) accommodation tends to be at the southern end of the resort, mainly along the West End Road. You can find a wide range, from classy hotels to tiny cabins or camping, including a variety of self-catering villas and rustic chalets. Many hotels have rooms in small blocks or cottages, and some offer cooking facilities as well as a restaurant.

Most attractive of the large, all-inclusive hotels along the northern part of Long Bay is **Swept Away** (tel: 957 4061), which is especially stylish, with suites and villas secluded in extensive tropical gardens beside the beach. In a similar price bracket is **Sandals Negril** (tel: 957 4216), which is in much the same vein as other Sandals hotels (such as in Montego Bay). Those in search of a hotbed of adult holiday fun and games, rather than a haven, could try the cheaper **Hedonism II** (tel: 957 4200). Next to it, at the south end of Bloody Bay, lies the opulent, sophisticated **Grand Lido** (tel: 957 4010), which is more formal than other Negril hotels. The only all-inclusive hotel here which caters for families with children is the **Poinciana Beach Resort** (tel: 957 4256). All these hotels have extensive facilites.

Point Village Resort (tel: 957 9170), on Rutland Point, has luxury studios and suites with kitchens – and lovely views. Facilities are good, including restaurants and children's activities.

Lying beside Long Bay beach, further south on Norman Manley Boulevard, are a range of comfortable hotels at moderate rates, offering a variety of amenities (including pools). The rather Spanish-style **Charela Inn** (tel: 957 4648) has a personal atmosphere; the **Negril Tree House** (tel: 957 4287) is in an appealing ethnic-style building, and it also has cottages; the **Negril Gardens** (tel: 957 4408) has a pretty pink and white colour scheme. More expensive is the quiet, small and neat **Sea Splash** (tel: 957 4041).

Secluded amongst the trees north of the airstrip, on the inland side of the road beside Bloody Bay, is the reasonably-priced **Negril Cabins Resort** (tel: 957 4350). Rooms are in wooden chalets on stilts, and it has a pool.

Straightforward self-catering cottages offering homely comfort and reasonable rates include **Yellow Bird Sea-Tel** (tel: 957 4252) and **Crystal Waters** (tel: 957 4284), both conveniently located on the beach. Budget self-catering rooms or cottages in the same area can be found at **The Golden Sunset** (tel: 957 4241) – it has a good restaurant by the beach. And the **Negril Yoga Centre** (tel: 957 4397) has a few rustic cabins and cottages set in gardens near the centre, across the road from the beach (some have cooking facilities).

Reasonably-priced accommodation along the West End Road includes **Rockhouse** (tel: 957 4373), which has romantic palm-thatched rondavel cottages clustered on the cliff-tops. They have hot plates for cooking, and there is also a restaurant; it has recently been refurbished, and now has a pool. **Rock Cliff** (tel: 957 4331) is a comfortable, friendly hotel

A romantic setting at Rockhouse

with a pool. Also set in gardens on the cliffs, the cottages at **Awee Maway** (tel: 957 4864) feature hammocks and waterbeds, and there is a thatched bamboo restaurant. Nearby is **Xtabi** (tel: 957 4336), a delightful retreat, with rooms and cottages (including cooking facilities), a pool and restaurant perched on the cliff-tops.
Good value for the budget-conscious can also be found at three places on the inland side of West End Road. **Thrills** (tel: 957 4390) is a small, lively hotel with a pool. Lying off the coast road, the attractive **Summerset Village** (tel: 957 4409) has a variety of charming villas (offering rooms or self-catering) set in gardens with a pool and restaurant. Next to it is the rustic, peaceful **Addis Kokeb Guest House and Cottages** (tel: 957 4485); self-catering is also available here.

Nightlife and Entertainment
There is a good choice of organised excursions (by boat, coach or horse) to see some of

the scenic spots around Negril as well as elsewhere on the island. These include trips that start in Montego Bay, like the **Appleton Express** (see page 24). Information can be obtained from hotels, booths on the beach or the Tourist Board office.
The pace of Negril hots up after the sun goes down. Organised evening excursions include sunset party cruises, where you can dance to live reggae, see a folk show or enjoy a barbecue. Many hotels have beach barbecues and entertainment; regular live reggae shows are held at the **SamSara**, **Negril Tree House** and **Summerset Village**. The **Charela Inn** has a folklore show. And there are hotel discos, for instance, at the **Negril Gardens**, **SamSara** and **Hedonism II**. Discos in the town centre include the funky **Compulsion** at the Plaza de Negril, and **Close Encounters** at Kings Plaza. Several restuarants and bars have live reggae, often

with top performers, once or twice a week – so every night there is a reggae show to be seen somewhere in Negril. A hot favourite is **Kaiser's Café**, down West End Road. Also along here is **MXIII**. Popular spots by the beach on Norman Manley Boulevard are **Alfred's** and **De Buss** (you can't miss the double-decker bus); nearby is **Risky Business**. (See also **Mandela's Green Entertainment Centre**, under **Restaurants**.) If that's not enough, reggae reigns supreme at Negril's annual **Reggae Festival** in March (see the Tourist Board for details and dates).

So much for the organised entertainment. But in Negril, there is always the chance of an impromptu beach party, which can be most fun of all.

Restaurants

Take pot luck and you will find all sorts of cafés and palm-thatched beach bars serving tasty snacks. An atmospheric and busy place to eat is **Rick's Café**, Lighthouse Road (tel: 957 4335), perched on the cliffs around the West End point. The blackboard menu includes a variety of fish dishes (not cheap), and you exchange money for beads to buy drinks at the bar.

Lots of the hotels have good restaurants, such as the **Charela Inn** (tel: 957 4648), which serves Jamaican and French dishes either on the patio by the beach or in the smart dining room. A little further north on Long Bay is **Cosmo's Seafood Restaurant and Bar** (tel: 957 4330), in a large wood and bamboo barn on the beach, open to the breezes, with big wooden tables and benches; it offers local fare at very reasonable prices in a relaxed atmosphere – a favourite with Jamaicans and tourists alike.

Several miles north of Negril, at a fishing village called Green Island, is **Mandela's Green Entertainment Centre**. There is a palm-thatched upper floor giving views over the bay, and it serves good Jamaican food at low prices. At night it regularly sheds its calm, peaceful aura, when it puts on excellent shows, such as live reggae music.

Shopping

Negril is much more limited for shopping than Montego Bay or Ocho Rios. The main craft market is the lively **Negril Craft Park**, behind the beach at its southern end (near the centre of the resort). Here there are lots of little huts, selling a plethora of colourful goods, such as tie-dyed clothes, hammocks, coral and shell jewellery, as well as T-shirts and fruit. On West End Road near the centre is a two-storey open-air **Craft Vendors' Plaza**. Near the airstrip to the north lies the **Rutland Point Craft Market**. There are also lots of craft and souvenir stalls along the beach.

The two main shopping complexes, near the central roundabout, are **Adrija Plaza** and **Plaza de Negril**, where there are a couple of shops selling duty-free goods; a short way down the West End Road are **Kings Plaza** and **Sunshine Village**. These plazas are the place to come if you are looking for banks, supermarkets or pharmacies.

For local art and crafts try **Gallery Hoffstead II** at Plaza de Negril (there is also a branch in the little town of Lucea, see page 35), **Geraldine Robins**, on West End Road, or **Le Bric à Brac** by the beach.

Sports

For those requiring more activity than just reclining on the beach, Negril has a wealth of watersports – offered by the larger hotels or several

Jahbah's Health Food, Negril

independent companies (the Tourist Board has an approved list). Almost any watersport you've ever wanted to try is available here, as Negril is the perfect location.

Horse-riding is also popular. And there is an 18-hole golf course at **Negril Hills**.

The larger hotels have various other sporting facilities. Some allow visitors to pay to use them – such as the **Swept Away Sports Complex**, which has an excellent range. For kids of all ages, **Anancy Park** (part of the Poinciana Beach Resort) has mini-golf, go-karts, nature trails, fishing and boating.

WHAT ELSE TO SEE IN THE NORTHWEST AND WEST

Calm and clear: Great River

♦♦♦
BELVEDERE ESTATE
In the midst of banana, citrus and coconut groves, this lush working plantation has recreated a quaint village from the last century, where artisans can be seen plying their crafts – such as the blacksmith and weaver. It also has a fascinating herb garden. The staff (dressed in period costume) explain bush medicine and describe life in the 19th century. Previously this was a sugar plantation, one of the first in Jamaica, and the ruined Great House dates back 300 years. There is an old sugar factory and hand-built dam which still harnesses the river waters. A garden walkway with labelled plants lies along the river, shaded by luxuriant foliage. You can take a cool dip in the limpid streams and waterfalls – as well as enjoy traditional food and music. About 15 miles (24km) south of Montego Bay.
Open: Monday to Saturday 10.00–16.00hrs.

♦
BLUE HOLE PLANTATION
On the steep slopes rising just inland of the coast, six miles (10km) east of MoBay, tours can be taken around this working plantation. All sorts of crops are grown here, such as bananas, ackee, coffee, pineapple and citrus fruits – which you will be able to sample. You can also look round the 18th-century Great House, and the old sugar mill and boiling house.
Open: daily 09.00–16.00hrs.

♦♦♦
COCKPIT COUNTRY
This haunting highland wilderness lies inland, southeast of Montego Bay, and rises to almost 2,500 feet (762m). The pockmarked *karst* plateau – with its caverns, sink holes, underground streams, tunnels, and craggy peaks cloaked in verdant vegetation – is best known as being the home territory of the Maroons. Various evocative names in this land of 'Me No Sen, You No Come', are reminders of the time when the

British rode back-to-back in pairs on one horse to try and avoid ambush: such as the District of Look Behind, Wait-A-Bit and Quick Step. Remote villages are scattered around its fringes, reached by narrow, winding, rough roads which offer some breathtaking views of the steep, forested slopes. But only a hiking trail crosses its rugged, untouched heart; and much is inaccessible except, perhaps, to intrepid explorers. High on the slopes of its southern side is the Maroon capital of Cockpit Country: a traditional village called **Accompong**. It is named after the brother of Cudjoe, who was leader of the First Maroon War. It was here, under a silk cotton tree, that they signed their peace treaty with the British. On Cudjoe Day, 6 January, it becomes a place of pilgrimage for the Maroons, and there are lively celebrations with much drumming and dancing. Normally this isolated village is a quiet place, its simple dwellings clinging to the jungly, rocky mountain sides – where the people are proud and friendly. Much of the pleasure of visiting it is for the drive there, through some spectacular scenery (either from the north or the south).

Southwest of Accompong are the **Ipswich Caves**, which have some striking stalactite and stalagmite formations. If you are interested in such geological wonders, the **Windsor Caves** are worth a visit – lying towards the uncharted depths of Cockpit Country on its northern flanks. The easiest way to explore

Cockpit Country is on the **Accompong Maroon Tour** from Montego Bay; the area can also be seen on other excursions, such as the **Appleton Express** which skirts its western rim and stops off at Catadupa and the Ipswich Caves (see page 24).

◆◆
CROYDON PLANTATION
This working pineapple and coffee plantation is set amid majestic mountain scenery, surrounded by slopes of tropical forest and tranquil valleys. It lies about 20 miles (32km) south of Montego Bay, by Catadupa, on the outskirts of Cockpit Country. A short guided walking tour explains some of its history, while showing modern cultivation and production techniques of various types of pineapple, other fruits, coffee and honey – you are given samples to taste. A popular way to see Croydon is on an organised excursion, which includes a barbecue lunch at the plantation.
Open: Monday to Saturday 09.00–15.30hrs.

◆◆
FALMOUTH
An appealing little town, on the flat coastal plain, 23 miles (37km) east of Montego Bay. It flourished as a sugar port from the late 18th century, but the port fell into disuse after the sugar industry declined and its harbour was unable to accommodate the new steam ships. Now rather scruffy, this adds to its unspoilt local character, with men mending

Greenwood recalls another age

nets by the sea and women selling wares on the street. It throngs with activity during the markets on Wednesday (selling clothing, fabrics and crafts), Friday and Saturday (for fruit and vegetables). You can see numerous examples of Georgian architecture around Market Street, just west of Water Square in the centre of town. Two notable old buildings include the **Courthouse**, dating from 1815 and the **Barrett House**, built by the sugar baron Edward Barrett. The rich and powerful Barrett family helped plan the town and owned several estates on the island.

A couple of miles (3km) east, by Rock, is a phosphorescent lagoon that looks luminous at night. There is a pleasant, inexpensive fish restaurant called **Glistening Waters** (tel: 954 2229) set directly on the deep bay, which also has a marina where you can take fishing charters or cruises. Alternatively, the small hotel **Rose's By The Sea** (tel: 954 4078) has a restaurant overlooking the lagoon, and also offers cruises.

Nearby, **Muriel Chandler's** shop sells vibrant batik cotton or silk clothing and fabric, and has a gallery of batik paintings.

◆◆◆
GREENWOOD GREAT HOUSE

Set on a hill above the coastal strip west of Falmouth, this fine old plantation house is built of stone and wood, with a shingle roof, and is surrounded by very pretty gardens. It dates from 1790, built by the poet Elizabeth Barrett Browning's family, who were one of the largest landowners in Jamaica. Their property included five Great Houses and 2,000 slaves. This estate extended 12 miles (19km) along the coast – of which there are wonderful views from the upper veranda along the back of the house. The elegant interior has many interesting and beautiful antiques. Some belonged to the Barretts, such as the library, Wedgwood china service and several carved wooden beds. The rest were collected by the present owners, including

some rare musical instruments. After the tour you can relax with a drink in the original kitchen which is now a bar. The house is about 16 miles (25km) east of Montego Bay.
Open: daily 09.00–17.00hrs.

◆
JAMAICA SAFARI VILLAGE
This open-air park is set in a mangrove swamp just west of Falmouth. Crocodiles, snakes and birds may be seen in their natural habitat, as well as small enclosures with various unhappy-looking animals, like the lioness. There are boat trips and refreshment facilities.
Open: daily 09.00–17.00hrs.

◆◆
LUCEA
Once a thriving sugar port, Lucea's harbour is one of the best on the north coast; now it mainly ships bananas and molasses – and fishing boats bring in their catches. On Saturdays, the town has a big, bustling market. Lucea has much unspoilt character, and it owes part of its picturesque charm to the old buildings along its narrow streets – including some stone and wood Georgian architecture and lots of cream-painted clapboard houses with 'gingerbread' fretwork around the balconies. By the central square – named after Alexander Bustamante (Jamaica's first Prime Minister) who was born near Lucea – is the 19th-century **Courthouse**. This cream wood building, with stone balustrades, has an unusual clock-tower supported by Corinthian-style columns, of

which Lucea is very proud. On a peninsula just to the north of the town, overlooking the harbour, is the dilapidated - 18th-century **Fort Charlotte**, named after George III's queen. Nearby, beside a big Catholic church, is the **Hanover Museum**, set right by the sea in the old British barracks. It contains displays of historical artefacts, including Arawak Indian tools and pots, and some interesting pictures. There is also a restaurant and visitors' shop.
Open: daily 09.00–18.00hrs.
From Lucea, you can drive up into the mountains for splendid panoramas and complete peace. Lucea lies 28 miles (45km) west of Montego Bay.

◆◆
MARTHA BRAE RAFTING
The Martha Brae River was named after a mythical Arawak Indian girl with supernatural powers. It flows into the luminous lagoon near Falmouth. The rafting trip starts at Rafters' Village three miles (5km) south, where there is a restaurant, bar, souvenir kiosks, picnic area, swimming pool, and children's play area. The bamboo raft glides down the meandering river, through low hills and lush green foliage, with only the 'splunk' of the rafter's pole in the sparkling water to break the peace. The trip takes an hour and a half and is a lovely way to see the unspoilt countryside and the flora, such as vine-tangled woods and fringes of feathery bamboo, as well as colourful birds and butterflies. The rafts

(which seat two people) run daily, 09.00 to 16.00hrs.

◆◆
MOUNTAIN VALLEY RAFTING
A raft trip along the Great River shows the inland countryside at its tranquil best. It starts high in the hills by the village of Lethe, several miles southwest of Montego Bay. For about an hour you are punted downstream in a bamboo raft, over gentle rapids and past spectacular scenery – where there are many exotic birds. It can also give you a glimpse of typical local life along the banks – such as women washing clothes or children bathing. You can take a dip in the clear, green water, and stop at a riverside bar for a drink; there is also an optional plantation tour and hayride.
Rafts run daily, 09.00 to 16.00hrs.

◆◆◆
ROCKLANDS BIRD SANCTUARY AND FEEDING STATION
In the steep, forested highlands near Anchovy, eight miles (13km) south of Montego Bay, is a small property owned by Lisa Salmon – fondly known as 'the bird lady'. She set up her bird feeding station here in 1958 – the area is noted for its rich birdlife. In the late afternoon she puts out food on the patio, and all sorts of native and migrating wild birds come to feed. The birds take seeds from your hand, and humming birds – like the delightful Doctor Bird (Jamaica's national emblem) – sip sugar-water from little bottles you are given

to hold. It's a fascinating experience, enhanced by Miss Salmon's lively knowledge of Jamaican birds.
Open: daily 15.15hrs to sunset (feeding starts between 15.30 and 16.00hrs) – children under five not admitted

◆◆◆
**ROSE HALL
GREAT HOUSE** ✓

This grandest of Jamaica's Great Houses is also renowned for the haunting legend of the 'White Witch', Annie Palmer. It was built around 1770, then fell into ruin during the last century, but was restored to its former glory in the 1960s. The symmetrical façade is striking, with its Palladian portico and balustraded terrace reached by two flights of steps. Inside it is graced by rich woodwork, and the owners have tried to recreate the original elegance and splendour of an 18th-century colonial manor. It is full of fine antiques and art treasures, collected from around the world – from French chandeliers to Chinese screens. In fact, it is far more opulent than most plantation houses would have been – but this always was the showcase among Great Houses.
The infamous Annie Palmer was a former mistress of Rose Hall. Legend has it that she was practised in the art of voodoo magic, and managed to kill off three husbands by poisoning, strangling and stabbing. She was also said to have taken slaves as lovers, murdering them when she got bored, and

Peace and quiet near Ocho Rios

entertained herself by watching slaves being tortured. Finally, when the slave rebellion started in 1831, she was killed – one story claims it was by an African witch doctor whom she had seduced – and her ghost (*duppy*) is said to haunt Rose Hall. The guides here are very knowledgeable and bring the history alive. There is a small restaurant, Annie's Pub and gift shop. About 10 miles (16km) east of Montego Bay.
Open: daily 09.00–18.00hrs.

◆
SEAFORD TOWN
Lying in the mountainous western interior, about 25 miles (40km) south of Montego Bay, this small place is best known for its community of German descendants. Peasant farmers from northern Germany settled here in the mid-19th century to cultivate sugar and bananas. The fair-skinned, blue-eyed inhabitants have preserved little of their culture (bar their surnames), and are about the only poor whites living in Jamaica. There is a small

historical museum by the old Catholic church.
Open: Monday to Saturday 10.00–16.00hrs.

CENTRAL NORTH COAST

This area covers the parishes of St Ann and St Mary, in the northern part of the county of Middlesex. It is here that Jamaica's second tourist mecca, Ocho Rios, lies – as well as the smaller resort of Runaway Bay.
The busiest stretch of the main road along the coast is west of Ocho Rios, continuing on to Montego Bay. Although development spreads either side of the resorts, parts of the coast are still unspoilt, particularly in St Mary. The coastal strip rises quickly to a sea of wooded hills and mountains inland, laced by verdant valleys. Close to the coast there is tree-scattered pastureland, and sugar cane, coconut, citrus and banana plantations.

As you go east, the coastal landscapes become increasingly interesting, with steep hills ascending directly from the cliffs and coves, and more extravagant, jungly vegetation – especially after you enter St Mary. In places, the coastline offers dramatic scenery and beautiful views; towards the east you begin to see the peaks of the Blue Mountains in the hazy distance. It is much less touristy and quieter as Ocho Rios is left behind.

The best beaches in this area are around Ocho Rios – coves of sparkling white sands. Beaches are generally shallower and more rocky around Runaway Bay. St Mary's coast tends to be rocky, with cliffs and beaches of grey shingly sand.

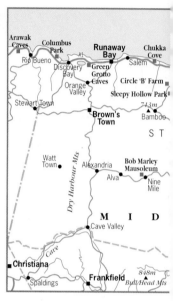

WHAT TO SEE

◆◆

OCHO RIOS

This thriving resort is said to derive its name from the Spanish *Las Chorreras* – referring to its waterfalls, especially the splendid **Dunn's River Falls** west of the town (see page 48). Whether the British misheard (or couldn't count), it came to be called Ocho Rios – meaning 'eight rivers' – now fondly known as Ochi by the locals. Whereas other north coast towns have declined from busy ports into quiet fishing villages, Ocho Rios has done the reverse, thanks to its development as a centre for tourism and shipping bauxite. In recent years, it has become Jamaica's prime cruise ship destination.

There are no historic buildings, except the remains of a late 17th-century **fort** with a couple of cannons, by the main road on the western edge of town – lying next to a dusty bauxite installation. Ochi boasts a very attractive setting: the centre lies behind Ocho Rios Bay, whose clear turquoise sea is bordered by a crescent of white sand. It is surrounded by a bowl of steep, green hills, luxuriantly clad in tropical vegetation. Ochi is full of fun – and commercialisation. The constant hum of people and traffic swells when a cruise ship arrives in town, with thronging tourists and locals touting for business. The resort is not subtle about the fact that it is very geared to visitors.

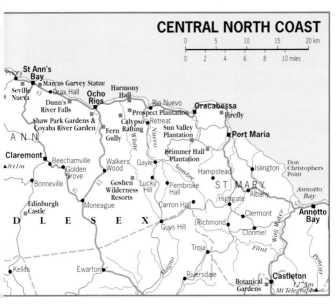

CENTRAL NORTH COAST

The area by Ocho Rios Bay is a hub of activity. The high-rise hotel blocks set around it are landmarks as you enter the resort. On the west side of the bay, near the bauxite terminal, is the cruise ship wharf. And when a gleaming luxury liner comes in, it is an impressive sight – sunbathers on the beach opposite have a front-row seat. Behind the beach is a large shopping complex, which includes the Tourist Board office, and the **Craft Market** is nearby. You can get a taste of real Jamaica in the **Vegetable Market**, which sprawls back from the main road near the clock tower.

Amid the noisy crowds inside, exotic (and familiar) fruit and

A flower lady in full bloom

Colourful sports at Turtle Beach

vegetables are piled in a rainbow of colours, from huge hanks of green bananas to scarlet peppers and orange pumpkins. The market also sells a wide variety of other items, including clothes. It is full of local atmosphere – not easy to find in Ochi – working up full steam by the end of the week.

For a wonderful panorama of the resort and the jungly hillsides rising behind the coast, visit **Shaw Park Gardens**, set on the steep slopes above the centre of Ocho Rios. It has acres of lush, landscaped grounds, brimming with beautiful flowers and birds. There are neatly-manicured gardens as well as wilder, wooded areas with bubbling streams and waterfalls.
Open: daily 07.30–17.30hrs.
Higher up the hill lies the picturesque **Coyaba River Garden and Museum**, whose tropical gardens feature waterfalls and fishponds; the museum has interesting displays showing Jamaica's history, it also has a local art gallery and good gift shop.
Open: daily 08.30–17.00hrs.

The central public beach (charging a small entrance fee) is **Turtle Beach**, a semi-circular curve of shimmering sand, with lots of facilities including watersports and bars. To the east of the resort, strips of silvery sand nestle in coves, between cliffs and rocky points thickly fringed with foliage. Most of these are private, for the guests of the hotels sitting behind them – but there is a stretch of public sand in the bay by the mouth of the White River (about three miles (5km) east). To the west is **Dunns's River Beach**, a delectable spot with Dunn's River Falls cascading down the hill behind – it can only be reached by paying to go into the grounds by the falls.

Accommodation
Ochi has a very wide range of accommodation, from eminently classy hotels to cabins and camping (in the resort and near Port Maria). Scattered along the coast to the east are several hotels secluded in verdant

gardens, beside private coves. Among the most elegant (and expensive) is the long-established **Jamaica Inn** (tel: 974 2514), serenely sophisticated and beautifully appointed, it has a personal atmosphere and old-world charm – in the past it entertained guests such as Noël Coward, Claudette Colbert and Winston Churchill. Further east, the delightful pastel pink and white **Sans Souci Lido** (tel: 974 2353) is extremely stylish; it is all-inclusive and has extensive spa facilities (one of the pools is fed by Sans Souci's own mineral spring). Closer to Ocho Rios on a hillside just inland, with its own beach on the coast below, is the large, luxurious, all-inclusive **Ciboney** (tel: 974 1027); it has villa suites, and is packed with sports and health facilities.

On the coast nearby is the rather less expensive **Plantation Inn** (tel: 974 5601), a tasteful, tranquil, very traditional hotel. Next to it is **Sandals Ocho Rios** (tel: 974 5691), an all-inclusive offering similar attractions to its sister hotels (such as in Montego Bay). **Sandals Dunn's River** (tel: 972 1610) is on the coast the other side of Ochi.

On a fine bay near the mouth of the White River to the east lies the **Shaw Park Beach Hotel** (tel: 974 2552), a lively, comfortable, standard modern hotel. Further east is **Couples** (tel: 975 4271), another all-inclusive, with lots of sports and activities for couples only. Near Oracabessa, **Boscobel Beach** (tel: 975 7331) is an all-inclusive aimed at families, with lots of activities for children (reminiscent of a fancy, tropical holiday camp).

Back in the centre of Ochi, there is plenty of reasonably-priced accommodation. Set behind Turtle Beach are two attractive, low-rise complexes of self-catering apartments, **Sandcastles** (tel: 974 5877), and **Fisherman's Point** (tel: 974 2837) – both have pools and restaurants. By the centre of the beach is **Club Jamaica** (tel: 974 6632), an intimate, upbeat all-inclusive hotel. Nestling in luxuriant gardens beside waterfalls, on slopes behind the centre of town, is **The Enchanted Garden** (tel: 974 1400), a peaceful and relaxing haven; it has suites or villas, a varied range of health facilities and activities, and a private area of beach (all-inclusive rates are available). Alternatives for the budget-minded include the homely and very appealing **Hibiscus Lodge** (tel: 974 2676), which has a rather Mediterranean atmosphere; it is not far from the centre, perched on cliffs (steps lead down to a bathing area), with pretty terraces, gardens and a pool. The **Little Pub Inn** (tel: 974 2324) is a lively guest house in the heart of town. About 20 miles (32km) east of Ocho Rios, near Port Maria, the **Casa Maria** (tel: 994 2323) is a small, quiet hotel set on slopes behind a picturesque bay, with a pool (the beach below is poor for bathing).

Nightlife and Entertainment

As you would expect, Ochi offers visitors a host of tours.

There are excursions all over the island, either by coach or helicopter – your hotel or the Tourist Board can give you details. Many of these excursions go to places listed under **What Else To See** on page 46) and for other areas of the island.

Boat trips along the coast often include lunch and snorkelling. There are popular 'party' cruises on an old wooden sailing schooner, in the daytime and evening – when the sunset and moonlight adds to the romance. For **An Evening on the White River**, you are taken by fishing canoe up the torchlit river, stopping for a buffet supper, entertainment including a folklore show, and dancing under the stars.

Ochi buzzes with life at night. The **Little Pub** on Main Street has live reggae every night, and puts on folklore shows with music and dance – it also has a restaurant (and late shopping). The weekly **Coyaba Moonshine Festival**, at the Coyaba River Garden, includes a Jamaican buffet and performances by jonkanoo dancers. The larger hotels have nightly entertainment; and there are discos at the **Shaw Park Beach Hotel**, the **Ciboney**, and the **Jamaica Grande** (by Turtle Beach). Alternatively, you can kick up your heels with the locals at the **Acropolis Disco** (in the Mutual Security Mall, 70 Main Street), or the **Roof Club** (on James Avenue).

The **Jamaica Carnival** is in April; and music comes to town in a big way during the **Ocho Rios Jazz Festival** in June.

Restaurants

If eating out, there is lots of choice here – from glamorous restaurants (especially in the smart hotels) to take-away burgers and fried chicken. Several hotels, both great and small, have good restaurants.

The **Almond Tree** at the Hibiscus Lodge, 83 Main Street (tel: 974 2676), is a popular place offering a good choice of tasty dishes at reasonable prices; and the ambiance is lovely, on an open-air terrace overlooking the sea.

The Ruins, DaCosta Drive (tel: 974 2789), has a pretty setting in gardens with sparkling waterfalls, near the centre; it is much frequented by tourists although the food is mediocre. If you decide to have more than a cocktail, try one of the Chinese specialities (it also has a cheaper fast-food section).

Evita's, Eden Bower Road (tel: 974 2333), is an old 'gingerbread' house perched on the hillside, with an outdoor terrace and fine vistas over the bay; the mouthwatering Italian menu (with imaginative Jamaican touches) ensures it is always busy.

On the banks of the White River, below the road bridge a couple of miles (3km) east of Ochi, is the **Jungle Lobster House** (no phone), an atmospheric Rasta restaurant serving brilliant food. The rickety wooden shack looks out over a cluster of fishing huts and canoes; on the earth floors inside are wooden tables with benches, and you can watch the fish, chicken and lobster being cooked on an open-flame stove, to the sound of reggae.

Further east lies **Harmony Hall** (tel: 975 4478), a picturesque 19th-century 'gingerbread' house (see page 51). The restaurant has an open-air patio by the garden, and offers a nice selection of local, oriental and American dishes.

Shopping

Ochi is a top favourite for shopping in Jamaica. There are several plazas with duty-free shops selling a wealth of goods. These include **Ocean Village**, behind the centre of the beach, which also has shops selling batik clothes, T-shirts, records and books; for local art and handicrafts visit **The Art Mart** or **Bibi's Collectibles**. In the **Taj Mahal Shopping Centre**, just down the road, the **Treasure Chest** sells Jamaican crafts and souvenirs.

Also in the centre, further east on Main Street, a good selection of shops can be found at **Soni's Plaza** (try **Calico Jack Treasures** for arts and crafts) and the **Island Plaza**. On

The Ruins Restaurant

the road going east out of Ochi is **Pineapple Place**, a complex of pink-painted shops, and further east lies **Coconut Grove**; you can buy duty-free goods, crafts and souvenirs at both shopping centres.

Adjacent to Ocean Village is the **Craft Market**, full of stalls selling a bright array of handicrafts – paintings, woodcarvings, shell and coral jewellery, drums and whistles, straw hats and baskets – as well as printed T-shirts or beaded hairbraiding. It is also worth having a look around the **Vegetable Market** (including stands on the pavements outside) for cheap souvenirs, from T-shirts to tambourines – best visited at the end of the week. Don't forget to haggle over your purchases at both markets.

The **Coyaba River Garden's** gift shop has some attractive and unusual local souvenirs. You can find some high-quality Jamaican art, crafts, gifts and a few antique items at **Harmony Hall**, east of Ochi.

Sports

There are all sorts of watersports facilities at larger hotels or **Turtle Beach**. Golf can be played at **Sandals Golf Club**, just inland. Horse-riding is also available, such as at **Chukka Cove Farm**, **Prospect Plantation** and **Sun Valley Plantation**. Polo can be watched at **Chukka Cove** and **St Ann's Polo Club**. Ask at your hotel or the Tourist Board for information.

◆

RUNAWAY BAY

Tradition has it that this is where the Spanish fled after their final defeat by the English. But the evocative name is just as likely to have come from the runaway

Fishy business at the Craft Market in Ocho Rios

slaves who took off to Cuba from here. It is claimed that both the Spanish and the slaves sought refuge in the nearby **Green Grotto Caves**. Whatever the truth, it is now a popular area for tourists to run away from the cares of the world. Runaway Bay has no real town or centre – it is a relatively recent resort development, spread along the coastal strip and main road – about 17 miles (27km) west of Ocho Rios and 50 miles (80km) east of Montego Bay. Along the coast are narrow stretches of sand and coral rocks. Green, wooded hills rise just south of the coast road, with views of mountains inland. The resort is quite simple and unpretentious; it lacks the elements of high-sophistication found in Montego Bay and Ocho Rios, and the unique style of Negril.

A few miles west lies **Discovery Bay**, a quiet little place which has better bathing than Runaway Bay.

Accommodation

The range of hotels is more limited than in the major resorts – and does not include any ultra-classy, ultra-expensive properties.

There are four all-inclusive hotels set by stretches of sand and low cliffs, with extensive facilities. The largest is **Jamaica-Jamaica** (tel: 973 2436), with an upbeat atmosphere and Jamaican theme extending from furnishings to food. The lively **Club Caribbean** (tel: 973 3507) has lots of little rondavel cottages lying amid tropical gardens. The **Franklin D Resort** (tel: 973 4591) is a pastel-pink complex with suites designed for families (all have kitchens), and good facilities for children. The most reasonably-priced accommodation is the **Eaton Hall Beach Hotel** (tel: 973 3404), whose main building was a 19th-century guest house; combining Spanish and English styles, it is rather smart with a personal atmosphere.

Beside patches of beach further west is the **Ambiance Jamaica** (tel: 973 2066), a comfortable, modern hotel at moderate rates, with a wide range of facilities for visitors.

For the budget-minded, the **Caribbean Isle** (tel: 973 2364) is a pleasant, friendly, quiet little hotel set by a strip of sand, with a pool.

Alternatively, try the **Runaway HEART Country Club** (tel: 973 2671), where young Jamaicans train to work in the tourist business; it lies in pretty gardens (with a pool), on a quiet hillside inland of the main road.

If you prefer self-catering accommodation, there is a wide variety. For example, **Sunflower Villas** (tel: 973 2173) offer some reasonably-priced and more luxurious villas, spread behind the beach and on an estate in the hills, with pools and various watersports (all-inclusive rates are available).

A few miles east of Runaway Bay are **Chukka Cove Villas** (tel: 974 2239), very well-appointed, up-market two-storey villas, set in peaceful, pretty gardens beside rocky coves, with a pool – by the Chukka Cove equestrian and polo centre.

Runaway Bay, where the sand and sea go on and on, thataway ...

Five miles (8km) west of Runaway Bay, at Discovery Bay, are the **Portside Villas and Apartments** (tel: 973 2007), overlooking the bay and beach; built in attractive Georgian style, they are well-equipped and comfortably furnished, with a pool and restaurant – at reasonable rates.

Nightlife and Entertainment

Runaway Bay is well located for visiting sights in the area and all over the island. Details of excursions are available from larger hotels. Many of the Ocho Rios-based tours are offered from here. You can take boat trips from hotel beaches.

The larger hotels have evening entertainment. There are also discos at **Jamaica-Jamaica**, **Club Caribbean** and the **Ambiance Jamaica**. A lively spot on Fridays and Saturdays is the 'underground' **Runaway Caves** disco, at the Green Grotto.

Restaurants

The choice around Runaway Bay is limited, although the hotels have restaurants. It is well worth trying the **Cardiff Hall**

restaurant at Runaway HEART Country Club (tel: 973 2671). The **Recovery** (no phone) is a typical, very simple little bar and restaurant, on the main road just west of the resort. It is a friendly place, serving large portions of delicious local food at low prices; the sounds of reggae and locals playing dominoes drifts through from the bar.

For jerk pork try **El Africano**, an open, wooden bar by the roadside between Runaway Bay and Discovery Bay.

The Portside Villas and Apartments in Discovery Bay has a restaurant called the **Sea Shanty** (tel: 973 2007), in a lovely setting on a wooden veranda built over the sea with views of the bay.

Ten miles (16km) east of Runaway Bay on St Ann's Bay, **The Mug** (tel: 972 1018) is also in a pretty position, with a pleasant breezy patio right on the sea; it is simple, good value and serves tasty local specialities including fish.

Shopping

Although there are a few shopping complexes, and some hotels have souvenir or clothes boutiques, generally shopping facilities are fairly basic. Shopping trips to Ocho Rios are run from several hotels and self-catering properties. Crafts are sold at stands beside the road, for instance around Salem, just west of Discovery Bay outside Columbus Park, and further west by Rio Bueno.

Sports

Again, larger hotels have plenty on offer – especially watersports. Diving is good here; there are schools at the **Club Caribbean** and **Ambiance Jamaica**, for example. The **Jamaica-Jamaica Golf Club** lies just inland. Horse-riding tours and events are available at **Chukka Cove Farm**.

WHAT ELSE TO SEE AROUND THE CENTRAL NORTH COAST

◆

BOB MARLEY MAUSOLEUM

In a remote mountain setting south of Runaway Bay – about 25 miles (40km) by narrow, potholed roads that wind sharply round the steep slopes – is the tomb of the reggae superstar and Rasta hero, Bob Marley, who died of cancer in 1981 (at the age of 36). A 55-mile-long funeral procession brought his body here, to the sleepy, rural settlement of Nine Mile, which is where Marley was born.

Although it is of limited interest to anyone who is not a fan, part of the pleasure of visiting it is the drive through beautiful, unspoilt countryside. At the bottom of the slope beneath the tomb is a café full of Rastas. They will take you up the hill to see where Marley was laid to rest. The Lion of Judah is depicted on the stained glass windows, and inside are pictures of Marley and Haile Selassie. Every 6 February they hold an all-night concert here, to celebrate Marley's birthday.

BRIMMER HALL PLANTATION

This plantation is in a lovely spot, with its bright white, 18th-century Great House perched on a hillside, surrounded by lush slopes covered in palm groves, sugar cane and green pastures. It is a working plantation and runs guided tours of its well-kept old estate, to show how the crops are cultivated and harvested – including coconuts, bananas, coffee, pineapples and sugar cane. Visitors are taken in a tractor-drawn jitney (open wagon), and the route passes not far from the houses where Noël Coward and Ian Fleming lived. Brimmer Hall has an attractive restaurant serving Jamaican specialities, a bar, souvenir shops and swimming pool. The plantation is about six miles (9km) southwest of Port Maria, 18 miles (29km) southeast of Ocho Rios.

Open: daily 09.00 to 17.00hrs; tours at 11.00, 13.30 and 15.30hrs (for about an hour).

BROWN'S TOWN

This quaint market town gives a vibrant taste of traditional rural Jamaica, just nine miles (14km) south of Runaway and Discovery Bay. It is clustered along valleys and up the surrounding hillsides, where colourful shacks cling to the steep slopes. Lining the main street are old wooden buildings with overhanging upper verandas and open fronts. The market is in full swing on Wednesday, Friday and Saturday, when the centre is crowded with stalls. You can see piles of fruit and vegetables, from ackee to oranges, yams or plantains; others selling clothes or household goods; a boy cutting sugar cane into lengths ready to be chewed; donkeys plod by with heavy loads; while tasty aromas waft from a fried fish shack painted Rasta colours. It is full of life and noise, with throbbing music and rumbling lorries.

CALYPSO RAFTING

This is an enjoyable way to see some of the scenery along the lower reaches of the White River. It starts just inland, up a lane running beside the river, a couple of miles (3km) east of Ocho Rios. From the bamboo raft you can appreciate the hills rising steeply on either side, smothered in green, jungle foliage which arches and drapes gracefully over the river. And you can stop for a dip in the cool waters. The trip down to the sea takes about 45 minutes. Rafts run daily, 09.00–17.00hrs.

◆
CIRCLE 'B' FARM

Lying uphill from the coast, this farm offers half-hour walking tours to see the wide range of crops (and livestock). Visitors can taste some of the produce, such as pineapples, bananas, citrus fruit, coconuts and watermelons, as well as vegetables like okra, callaloo (spinach) and cucumbers. The farm also provides a lunch of typical Jamaican dishes, and it has a bar and picnic area. Set almost halfway between Runaway Bay and Ocho Rios, a couple of miles (3km) to the south of the coast road.
Open: daily 10.00–17.00hrs.

◆
DISCOVERY BAY

Columbus is believed to have landed in this splendid, sheltered bay, which has palm-wooded hills rising behind and curving around to the western headland. It is dominated by a big bauxite plant and terminal, covered in red dust – visitors say it can be interesting watching the ships negotiating the coral reefs as they enter the bay.

Set high above the sea, on the cliff-tops to the west, is **Columbus Park**, an open-air museum (displaying canons and relics from sugar mills) with panoramic views over the bay. The resort itself is small and quiet – by the shore here is a restaurant, the **Sea Shanty** (see page 46). On the east side of the bay is the public beach of **Puerto Seco** (Dry Harbour – as named by Columbus), a stretch of sugary sand which is better for swimming than beaches around Runaway Bay, as it is less shallow and rocky underwater – some watersports are available here (there is a small entrance fee to the beach). Discovery Bay lies five miles (8km) west of Runaway Bay.

◆◆◆
DUNN'S RIVER FALLS ✓

Of Jamaica's many delightful waterfalls, these are the most famous – they are, in fact, a major attraction. But despite its popularity the site avoids feeling too commercial. Cool mountain waters cascade dramatically over smooth limestone rocks and terraces, into bubbling pools – altogether tumbling 600 feet (183m) to where it streams under the main road onto a beautiful beach below. The falls are bordered by overhanging trees and bright shrubs and there is a park on the hill alongside, with snack bars and craft shops.

A favourite sport is to climb the falls: starting from the beach, visitors climb in a group, all holding hands in a chain, led by a guide who carries everyone's cameras around his neck and shouts encouragement. It takes about half an hour and is great fun. The short climb is mostly quite gentle, although it is steep in a few places, and you have to watch for slippery rocks or strong torrents of water – you can make your exit early if it becomes too tiring. Otherwise you can watch these amusing antics from wooden platforms beside the falls. Climbers will get very wet, so swimwear is

See the light at Discovery Bay

essential (and shoes like trainers might be useful for protection against the rock) – there are changing rooms and lockers for your clothes and valuables on the beach. The falls lie about three miles (5km) west of Ocho Rios.
Open: daily 08.00–17.00hrs.

◆
FERN GULLY
Climbing up the steep hills just south of Ocho Rios, the main road snakes along the path of an old river bed. The sheer, rocky sides are carpeted by hundreds of species of ferns, while tall trees form a green canopy over the road, festooned with creepers and long trailing vines. The sunlight suddenly seems very bright when you leave the deep, cool shade of Fern Gully. Along the road are several craft vendors touting their wares. Tours often drive a couple of miles on up to the Swansea refreshment centre on a grassy hilltop, which has a bar – and glorious panormas of rugged, wooded mountains stretching into the distance.

◆◆◆
FIREFLY ✓

On a plateau, about 1,000 feet (300km) above the coast, is the surprisingly modest little house that Noël Coward had built in 1956. The witty playwright and composer spent much time here and entertained many famous guests. The absolutely divine views inspired his song, *A Room With A View*.
You can see right along the coastline, with bays and headlands where the forested hills plunge down to the sea. No wonder Coward fell in love with this place. The house has been restored to look much as it did when he lived here in the 1950s. You can see his two baby grand pianos, writing desk, and various memorabilia like manuscripts, music scores, paintings, records, even his clothes. There is also a display of archive photographs. In the garden is Coward's grave. The house is reached up a steep lane, off the main coast road about four miles (6km) east of

Splashing out at Dunn's River Falls

Oracabessa, 17 miles (27km) east of Ocho Rios.
Open: daily, 08.30–17.30hrs.
On the hill just below Firefly is an old stone building which is believed to have been Henry Morgan's 'pirate lair'; it has been renovated and is now a bar and gift shop. This spot was called Look-Out, before Coward christened it after the fireflies that twinkled all around when he first visited it. Further down the road, near the sea, is Goldeneye, the house Ian Fleming owned for nearly 20 years and where he invented James Bond. It is closed to the public.

◆◆
GOSHEN WILDERNESS RESORTS
Amid a sea of green mountains and peaceful valleys is the old coffee and sugar plantation of Goshen. Later the land was given over to rearing cattle and horses, and it is still a working cattle ranch. But the main attraction for visitors are the facilities for fishing. On the large estate are over 40 fish ponds, teaming with tilapia (fresh-water snapper) – which are grown commercially. Guides will help you bait your hook and throw your line. You can even have your fish cooked, and served in the restaurant with bammy (fried cassava bread) and festival (crispy dumpling), Jamaican-style. There is plenty to amuse all the family, including a boating pond, duck ponds, and a zoo where children can feed the sheep and goats. Otherwise, simply enjoy the beautiful scenery – sauntering along the hiking trail, or lazing in one of the thatched huts. It lies about 12 miles (19km) southeast of Ocho Rios.
Open: daily 10.00–17.00hrs.

◆
GREEN GROTTO CAVES
These limestone caves, whose passageways stretch for miles, are said to have given refuge to the Spanish, runaway slaves and pirates. The caverns feature a variety of extraordinary stalactite and stalagmite formations – some are hollow and the guide plays primitive 'tunes' on them with a stick. You will also see bats hiding in the nooks and crannies. The Green Grotto – so-called because of the green algae on the rocks – lies 120 feet (36m) underground. It is an eerie, vaulted chamber containing a lake, on which you can take a boat trip; this underground tidal

lake is a mixture of fresh and salt water, and is inhabited by fish (including crayfish and mullet) which are blind. Inside the entrance of the caves is a small bar and souvenir stands. The tour covers about a mile (1.6km), and takes around 45 minutes. Outside the caves is a 160 foot (49km)-deep lagoon. The caves are around two miles (3km) west of Runaway Bay.
Open: daily 09.00–17.00hrs.
On Friday and Saturday nights, the caves echo to the sounds of the **Runaway Caves** disco.

◆◆
HARMONY HALL

This very pretty 'gingerbread' house is a restored Victorian manse dating from 1886, which was part of a pimento estate. Built of stone and white-painted woodwork, with a green shingled roof and pointed tower, it has exquisite lacy wooden fretwork around the eaves and upper veranda, referred to as gingerbread fretwork. Outside steps lead up to the veranda where there is an art gallery and craft shop on the first floor. There are displays of some wonderful work by contemporary Jamaican artists,

as well as high-quality crafts and gifts; it also has special exhibitions. On the ground floor and garden patio is a pleasant restaurant (see page 43). It is located by the main coast road about four miles (6km) east of Ocho Rios.
Open: daily (gallery 10.00–18.00hrs; restaurant and bar noon–22.00hrs).

◆
ORACABESSA

This little, local port gained its name from the Spanish (*ora* and *cabeza*, meaning Golden Head), and it sits on a green, wooded hillside, to one side of a creek. It is a typical sleepy village of wooden buildings – some with lacy fretwork around the verandas, many rather rickety. Just to the northeast is a track leading to the sea (opposite a petrol station), where there is a pocket-handkerchief-sized sandy beach which is very sheltered. Traditional fishing canoes and fishing cages lie on the beach; it also has a simple refreshment shack. Oracabessa is located 13 miles (21km) east of Ocho Rios.

The view from Firefly

Heading east of here, you will see some of Jamaica's finest coastal landscapes.

PORT MARIA

This bustling town is set above a huge, rocky bay, and there are views of the coastline with its splendid headlands and verdant hills. Once a busy banana port, it is now a market and fishing town. In the shopping centre, the streets are lined with stalls, fruit and vegetables are piled high on the pavement; a big market is held here on Friday and Saturday. A bridge joins this part to a quieter residential area, where goats nibble the greenery beside the road. Near the 19th-century church, a sign directs you to the Tacky Monument, dedicated to the leader of the 1760 slave rebellion.

North of town, an open, palm-thatched jerk chicken bar by the sea offers lovely views of the quiet bay.

Port Maria lies 21 miles (34km) east of Ocho Rios.

♦♦♦
PROSPECT PLANTATION

This is one of the most popular plantation tours. It combines a glimpse of spectacular scenery, including forested hills, mountains and valleys, as well as interesting information on the crops and plants of Jamaica, and some of the island's history. The huge estate covers about 1,000 acres (400 hectares); visitors are taken round in a tractor-drawn jitney (open wagon), to be shown crops like pineapples, sugar cane, bananas, coffee, cassava, pimento (allspice), coconuts, cocoa, pawpaw and other fruit. The guides are very knowledgeable, and make the trip entertaining – climbing a tree to pick a coconut, giving you samples to taste or spicy leaves to smell. You will also learn about some of the exotic trees and flowers; lots of the trees here have been planted by famous visitors, and bear plaques with names like Noël Coward, Winston Churchill, Prince Philip and Charlie Chaplin. It is a peaceful (if rather bumpy) ride and worth it for the dramatic views – including the White River Gorge, where you can see the river rushing over rocks far below the sheer hillsides festooned with foliage. And from Sir Harold's Viewpoint there are splendid panoramas of the hills, coastline, and the early 18th-century Great House, where the owner Lady Mitchell (Sir Harold's widow) lives.

Apart from the tour (which takes about an hour), you can take horse rides around the plantation (book an hour in advance). The estate also has an 18-hole mini-golf course, and a bar at the entrance.

Prospect lies just off the main road, about four miles (6km) east of Ocho Rios.
Open: daily, tours Monday to Saturday 10.30, 14.00 and 15.30hrs, Sunday 11.00, 13.30 and 15.00hrs.

♦
RIO BUENO

Once a busy port, now an appealing fishing village, the

Prospect Plantation – glorious scenery and fascinating history

horseshoe-shaped bay also has claims on being the site where Columbus first landed. There are several architectural reminders of past colonial days. **Gallery Jo James** has paintings and woodcarvings, as well as a simple restaurant. There is also a roadside stop with stands selling souvenirs and crafts. Just west of here are the **Arawak Caves**, with wall paintings and artefacts of the island's first inhabitants.

Rio Bueno lies six miles (9km) west of Discovery Bay.

◆
ST ANN'S BAY

This town is set on the slopes rising inland of the main road, which runs beside the big, sheltered bay. In the distance you can see a line of white waves in the turquoise sea, where they break on the coral reef. The palm-covered hills behind the bay ascend to mountains inland. Along the narrow streets in town are typical old clapboard buildings with upper verandas forming arcades over the pavements. It is a busy shopping centre, and market stalls and piles of produce line one of the steep central streets. It was here that Marcus Garvey was born, and his **statue** stands in front of the library. The town also has an 18th-century fort and 19th-century courthouse. Beside the bay is a simple little restaurant, **The Mug** (see page 46). The town lies seven miles (11km) west of Ocho Rios.

Just west of St Ann's Bay is the site of **Sevilla la Nueva** (or **Seville Nueva**), the Spanish colonists' first settlement. It was founded in 1509 by a son of Columbus – and abandoned in 1534. The scant ruins are now being excavated, and include the oldest church in the western hemisphere. They lie on the estate of Seville Great House,

which has an exhibition of
Spanish and Arawak artefacts
found at the site.
Open: daily 09.00–17.00hrs.
Nearby is a statue of
Columbus – who was forced to
spend over a year here, after
his ships sank in the bay
in 1503.
To the east of St Ann's Bay is
Drax Hall, where there is a
pretty, palm-fringed, sandy
beach called **Mammee Bay**.
St Ann's Polo Club also lies
nearby.

◆◆
SLEEPY HOLLOW PARK
Nestling in a valley below
verdant mountain slopes, this
delightful spot lives up to its
name. The park offers a
variety of attractions: you can
take tranquil walks to a river,
watch the colourful birdlife, go
pond-fishing, or look around
the herb and vegetable
gardens. Children will enjoy
the playground and donkey
rides. There is also a bar and
grill. It lies almost halfway
between Runaway Bay and
Ocho Rios, three miles (5km)

south of Priory on the main
coast road.
Open: daily 10.00–18.00hrs.

◆◆
SUN VALLEY PLANTATION
A luscious profusion of tropical
fruits are grown on the
picturesque valley slopes and
hillsides of this plantation,
which has been working for
250 years. Visitors can learn
about some of its interesting
history while being shown
round the estate by the family
owners. You will be taken for a
stroll along the 'banana walk',
visit waterfalls which you can
climb, and sample some of the
exotic fruit. There is a bar to
relax in afterwards, where
tempting cocktails are mixed
for you. Horse riding around
the plantation can also be
arranged. It is a few miles south
of Oracabessa, 16 miles (25km)
southeast of Ocho Rios.
Open: Monday to Friday, tours
at 09.00, 11.00 and 14.00hrs
(horse riding daily, book an
hour in advance).

Scuba diving at St Ann's Bay

THE NORTHEAST

Boundbrook Wharf at Port Antonio

This small area, mostly lying in the parish of Portland – the northern part of the county of Surrey – boasts some of the best Jamaica has to offer. It is much less touristy than other parts of the north coast, with one resort, Port Antonio.

Here there is some of the island's most stunning scenery, both along the coast and inland. The rugged coast sweeps up to voluptuous hills, rising to the high inland peaks of the Blue Mountains, which are usually bathed in misty clouds. The northeast tradewinds, meeting the high land, sprinkle more rain in this area than elsewhere on the island. Consequently the tropical foliage is at its most vibrant and lavish. The hills are cut by deep valleys and gullies,

as many rivers tumble from the mountains to the sea. All around the northeast you encounter endless breathtaking views of the coastline and mountains inland. The western part of this coast is indented with bays – where there are often sleepy little fishing villages, their canoes drawn up on the beach. High, wooded headlands plunge directly down to the sea, with cliffs in many places. There are banana plantations and coconut groves along the coast, as well as pastures with cattle grazing.

The landscapes are especially striking just east of Port Antonio, where picturesque coves pepper the coast, backed by steep slopes shrouded in the most profuse and verdant vegetation. This part has some of the island's loveliest beaches, which are invitingly unspoilt. Although the coast west of here has beaches of grey shingly sand and rocks, around Port Antonio the sand becomes pale and silvery again. The east is more windswept, with surf-splashed cliffs and waves rolling in to deserted stretches of sand. This is an area to visit if you want peace and quiet. But despite being very low-key compared to other northern resorts, Port Antonio does have a sophisticated side to it that is missing on the south coast (apart from Kingston).

WHAT TO SEE

◆◆◆
PORT ANTONIO ✓

This could well claim to be Jamaica's most enchanting coastal resort town. In the early days, the rugged terrain and thick jungle deterred extensive settlement in this part of the island. Port Antonio started expanding in the late 19th

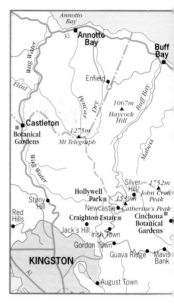

century, when the banana trade began. By the 1920s and 1930s, this had become the world's banana capital. It started

Taking the banana trail – bamboo rafts which once carried fruit are now a tourist's treat

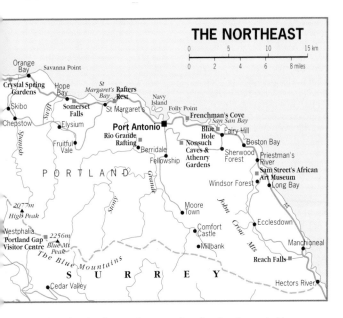

THE NORTHEAST

declining shortly afterwards, partly because of the devastating effects on the crops of Panama Disease and the hurricanes. Bananas were carried down the Rio Grande on bamboo rafts – which are now used to transport tourists instead. In Port Antonio's heyday, locals carried huge bunches of bananas on their heads, singing to help them bear the heavy loads and hard work – like the 'Banana Boat Song' made famous by Harry Belafonte.

Port Antonio was a popular spot with visitors long before Montego Bay or Ocho Rios. The development of tourism at the beginning of the century was closely linked with the banana trade: an enterprising entrepreneur started bringing North American passengers to Port Antonio on the empty banana boats that were coming to collect their cargo. Later, it thrived as a romantic hideaway for movie stars and other fashionable luminaries, such as Errol Flynn, Bette Davies, Clara Bow, Ginger Rogers, William Randolph Hearst and Rudyard

Kipling. Flynn sailed here on his yacht in the 1940s, fell in love with Port Antonio (as many do) and bought Navy Island; his reputation for hellraising and wild parties has entered the annals of local legend. His widow has remained here, living on a large ranch to the east. Port Antonio is still a relaxed haven, with an air of exclusivity enduring from the days when it entertained a glittering élite. But you do not have to be either rich or famous to share its treasures. Port Antonio combines unspoilt local character with a good range of amenities for visitors, in a very appealing manner.

An important part of this special charm is due to its beautiful setting. It sits beside superb twin harbours, flanked by Navy Island, nestling in the close embrace of luxuriantly wooded hillsides, with a backdrop of soaring, blue-tinged mountain peaks. Rivers flow into both **West** and **East Harbour**, and the busy centre lies behind the harbours. Jutting out between these two deep, sheltered bays is a peninsula bluff on which the quieter residential district of **Titchfield** lies. It was once the most exclusive part of town – and there are some fine examples of Victorian 'gingerbread' houses here. Around the town can be seen typical, clapboard buildings, their balustraded upper verandas (some decorated with gingerbread fretwork) shading the streets below. At the junction of Harbour Street and West Street is a square with a clock tower and an old red-brick **courthouse**, its white stone-work, columns and wrought-iron veranda sparkling in the sun. Just up Harbour Street, in the City Centre Plaza, is the local Tourist Board office; further along is **Christ Church**, an imposing stone Anglican parish church, dating from 1840. West Street is the main thoroughfare lying behind West Harbour. In a big building, opposite a little square with a cenotaph monument, is the **Town Market** which is packed with piles of colourful fruit (including different varieties of banana) and vegetables, as well as some crafts and gifts; the best market days are towards the end of the week. Also on West Street is the entrance to the **Huntress Marina**, where there are sleek yachts and deep-sea fishing boats moored beside the jetty – on which is a palm-thatched bar, ideal for sitting to watch the activity in the harbour. Port Antonio is renowned for its deep-sea fishing, especially blue marlin.

Nearby you can take the quaint little passenger ferry (the service runs day and night) to **Navy Island** – which was sold by Mrs Errol Flynn after her husband died, but is still privately owned. Nothing remains of the large naval station that the British built here long ago. It is a pretty little wooded island, where there are several small sandy beaches. Flynn's residence is now the Navy Island Marina Resorts hotel (with an Errol Flynn Memorabilia Room); it has a restaurant, beach bars and a marina offering watersports.

Port Antonio's West Harbour

Little fishing canoes are pulled up on the mainland shore, beside the road curving around East Harbour. The north side of the harbour is protected by another peninsula, on which is the **Folly Estate**. A track leads to the ruins of a stone and concrete mansion, with grand Doric columns and dubious graffiti. The views across the harbour to Port Antonio, with the Blue Mountains behind, provide more to look at than the building. It was built in 1905 by a rich American, for his wife who was one of the Tiffanys of New York. Local legend has it that he stocked the gardens with flowers, birds and animals – all white – but when he carried his bride over the threshold, the mansion started collapsing and his wife fled. The truth is much more prosaic: they both lived here periodically in the latter years of their life, and it was in the late 1930s that the roof collapsed as the salty air corroded the reinforcement rods. Nearby, standing on the end of the peninsula, is the 100-year-old Folly Point Lighthouse. The main road continues east, hugging the coast where waves crash against the rugged coral and volcanic rocks in plumes of spray. On a headland next to one of Jamaica's loveliest hotels, the Trident, is a massive, white, Christmas-cake-style 'castle'. Locals called it Folly II, as it lay unfinished for several years in the early 1980s, when the baroness who had it built ran into problems (she also built the Jamaica Palace hotel nearby). It was rescued by the architect who designed the Trident, and the mansion is used as his country abode.

Further east, a little road leads down to **Frenchman's Cove**. The hotel has still not been repaired after being damaged by Hurricane Gilbert in 1988, but you can pay a small charge to use this gem of a beach. The little cove of creamy sand is sheltered by jungle-clad cliffs, and a limpid, green stream meanders around the edge into the sea. The beach shelves quite steeply underwater, so the undertow can be strong; but in places the stream is deep enough to bathe in, as it runs over the sand.

A little further east is **San San Beach**, which is a public beach (with a small admission charge). In the bay of streaked turquoise sea lies a minute islet crowned in a profuse clump of trees – Monkey Island. The beach has a variety of facilities, including a restaurant, bar, watersports and lifeguard.

Along this winding coastal road, you will pass a couple of sleepy villages snuggled amongst the lush greenery. Sitting on the steps of one of the open-fronted bar-shops, visitors are treated to a colourful soap-opera of local life unfolding in the main street. The prettily named Fairy Hill is one such village; and down a precipitous rough track is **Fairy Hill Beach** (or **Winefride's Beach**). It is a delightful, secluded spot – little known except to locals, and a few who travel from Kingston at weekends to visit it. The weathered skeleton of a tree lies on the sand, and children play in its branches. The tranquillity is broken only by the soothing sound of waves breaking on the reef in the bay – except when locals hold a party here on Saturday night.

Accommodation

The choice here is much more limited than in the major resorts. But it does have a reasonable range - from some plush hotels and villas secluded along the coast, to simple hotels and guest houses, and even camping near Buff Bay.

The **Trident Villas and Hotel** (tel: 993 2602) is outstandingly classy (with prices to match); it occupies a fine position on a rocky headland just east of town, next to a tiny private sandy cove. Tastefully designed throughout, it has beautifully stylish, spacious villas set by the crashing waves, in immaculate gardens with strutting peacocks. It is quite small, with a serene and personal atmosphere.

Less expensive is the attractive **Navy Island Marina Resorts** (tel: 993 2667), a small hotel with cottages sprinkled over the pretty island, and various sports facilities (see also page 58).

East of the Trident, along the coast are four very different, moderately-priced hotels. Sitting in imposing splendour on the inland side of the road overlooking a rocky bay, is the **Jamaica Palace Hotel** (tel: 933 2020); opulent and classical in style, with a Middle Eastern flavour, it has a Jamaica-shaped pool in the gardens. The gleaming white villa perched on lush slopes nearby is the slightly cheaper **Mockingbird Hill Hotel** (tel: 993 3370), which is small and intimate, with a pool and spectacular views. High on the steep, verdant hillside behind San San Bay is the **Fern Hill Club** (tel: 993 3222); it has rooms in plantation-style houses and villas, including some suites with private spa pools on the balcony, with a wide range of amenities and activities. **Dragon Bay Beach Resort** (tel: 993 3281) has villas (self-catering available) clustered in picturesque gardens beside its own sandy cove; facilities include a thatched beach restaurant and a variety of sports.

On a hilltop, 600 feet (183m) above Port Antonio, with stupendous panoramas of its harbours and the mountains to the south, is the **Bonnie View Plantation Hotel** (tel: 993 2752). It lies in the grounds of a working plantation, and is one of the oldest hotels in the Caribbean; modest but homely, at very reasonable rates, it has a pool and horse-riding.

Old-fashioned, simple accommodation is found at the family-run **DeMontevin Lodge** (tel: 993 2604), in a quaint old Victorian 'gingerbread' house on the peninsula between Port Antonio's two harbours.

There are some lovely self-catering villas (with cooks provided if required) nestling on the tropical hillsides around San San Bay, where the views are magnificent. **Goblin Hill** (tel: 925 8108) is a white stucco, Georgian-style villa complex with a pool and sports. **San San Villas** (tel: 974 2508 to book) include a variety of properties in the area – some are very luxurious, with pools.

Nightlife and Entertainment

The **Navy Island Beach Buffet** is a lively evening of folk-dancing and fire-eating, along with an open-air dinner. The **Fern Hill Club** puts on nightly entertainment such as folk shows, beach parties or live reggae (with dinner, at an all-in price). **Shadows** is an upmarket nightspot in town (on West Street). There is also a disco at the **Mango Tree** (Sommers Town Road). But if you want to get-on-down with the locals, go to the funky **Roof Club** (West Street), where the reggae is throbbingly loud.

There is much merrymaking in August during the **Portland Jamboree**, with street parades and dancing, beach parties, cabaret shows, and a host of cultural and sporting events (contact the Tourist Board for details and dates).

Restaurants

Several of the hotels mentioned above have restaurants worth trying. Home-style local dishes

The pool at Jamaica Palace Hotel

at budget-prices are offered by the **Bonnie View Hotel** (tel: 993 2752), with its splendid views, and the **DeMontevin Lodge** (tel: 993 2604), whose owner used to cook for Errol Flynn. The **Navy Island Marina Resorts** (tel: 993 2667) has a popular restaurant in an attractive setting. For the ultimate in elegant dining, visit the *soigné* restaurant at the **Trident Hotel** (tel: 993 2602). (Make advance reservations for the latter three restaurants.) In town there is a variety of small restaurants serving Jamaican fare. Among these is **Daddy Dee** (no telephone) on West Street, a friendly, local bar where you can eat well and cheaply.

For jerk pork or chicken, go to Boston Bay.

Shopping

This is not Port Antonio's long suit, although there are plenty of shops to fulfil everyday needs. The **City Centre Plaza**, on Harbour Street, has a shop selling duty-free items such as crystal, china and jewellery. The **Oasis**, in Harbour Street, has Jamaican wood and wickerwork, T-shirts, jams and books. The **Crafts Market** can be found at the back of the busy Town Market on West Street – best visited on Friday or Saturday – where you can buy wood carvings, straw baskets, sandals, T-shirts as well as exotic fruit and spices. Next to the Jamaica Palace Hotel is a woodwork and craft centre; and at Fairy Hill, further east, is a roadside shack selling a variety of wicker items.

The famous DeMontevin Lodge is an architectural gem

Sports

Some of the hotels have a variety of facilities, including watersports – which are also available from **San San Beach** or the **Huntress Marina**. Deep-sea fishing is excellent in the waters off Port Antonio; an international Spring Fishing Tournament (in March) and International Marlin Tournament (in October) are held here.

There is a nine-hole golf course at **San San Country Club**. The area also offers horse-riding, and mountain bike rides down the slopes of the Blue Mountains.

WHAT ELSE TO SEE IN THE NORTHEAST

◆
ANNOTTO BAY

The name of this town comes from an orange dye made from a tropical tree that used to grow here. It is a pleasant place, set on a wide bay, where two estuaries flow into the sea. Women can be seen kneeling on the shingle beach, doing their washing in the river. The

Two views of Blue Hole's deep and translucent waters

normal sleepy pace of local life here becomes colourfully lively on Saturdays, market day, when all sorts of exotic fruit and vegetables grown in this fecund area are on sale. Annotto Bay lies 29 miles (47km) west of Port Antonio.

◆◆
BLUE HOLE

Also known as the Blue Lagoon, for reasons that become clear as its waters when you see it. The lagoon, of translucent, emerald–turquoise water, is set on the rocky coast to one side of San San Bay with its lovely beach – six miles (10km) east of Port Antonio. Luxuriant, dark-green jungle cloaks the sheer slopes rising all around, shading the lagoon which is reputed to be bottomless, although realists estimate around 200 feet (60m). You can swim in the waters, feeling the warm sea mixing with the cold springwater that feeds it. The romantic say it has a rejuvenating effect, but if you bathed in all the waters in Jamaica that are supposed to have that effect, you would be back in your second childhood before long.

From the lagoon, visitors can take a glass-bottomed boat trip (or raft) round to San San Beach and Monkey Island, a pretty little blob of jungle lying in the bay.

◆◆◆
BOSTON BAY

Connoisseurs claim this is *the* place to try Jamaica's jerk pork, and it is because of this reputation that jerk pork is often prefixed with 'Boston' at snack

THE NORTHEAST

stands all over the island. It is sold by the pound, and can be very fatty, so specify what you want (if unsure, ask to try before you buy). This is a busy, popular spot with locals around lunchtime. You can also buy jerk chicken, spicy sausage, festival (a crispy, deep-fried dumpling), and cold drinks to quench the fire of the piquant pork. It may not be to everyone's taste, but the beach certainly is. The beautiful bay of shimmering, silvery sand is set between golden cliffs, and surrounded by trees. The brilliant aquamarine sea is good for swimming – or surfing, on the sizeable waves that roll into the bay. Boston Bay is nine miles (14km) east of Port Antonio.

CASTLETON GARDENS

Not only are these botanical gardens a rich showcase of tropical flora, but the drive there is magnificent – as it lies almost halfway to Kingston along the 'Junction' road, in the mountainous interior. The road follows the ravine of the Wag Water River, winding precipitously round hairpin bends (watch out for buses coming thundering round the corners). Streams and waterfalls tumble down the sheer rocky sides, the slopes soar up to the Blue Mountains in the east, and the landscape is covered in a high, tangled canopy of rain forest. Castleton Gardens were established in 1862, covering 15 acres (6 hectares) of what was once a sugar plantation. There are over 1,000 different species of native and exotic

plants in the gardens, including many imported from South America – with 47 varieties of palm, many pretty shrubs and flowers. It is worth hiring the services of guide Roy Bennett (who learnt about the gardens from his father, who was a guide before him). He knows all the plants like the back of his hand – on which he will demonstrate how the tattoo fern leaves a white imprint of its feathery leaves. He will show you flowering trees like the blue mahoe (giant hibiscus, which is Jamaica's national tree) and flame of the forest, plants that produce camphor, eucalyptus, nutmeg, allspice, even strychnine; and he will also point out beautiful birds, as he knows where their favourite spots are. You can bathe in the crystal-clear river, or picnic on the shady banks, watching butterflies flutter about the gardens. There is a small bar. It lies southwest of Port Antonio, 12 miles (19km) south of Annotto Bay, and about 18 miles (29km) north of the centre of Kingston.
Open: daily 08.00–18.00hrs.

CRYSTAL SPRINGS

The land here was once a sugar cane plantation, and is now a centre for 'ecotourism' (the story of Jamaica's economy in a nutshell). It is a recreational area where visitors can enjoy the natural environment. The botanical gardens boast a brilliant array of exotic orchids. There is also a tropical bird sanctuary, apiary, and pretty picnic area. It offers overnight

accommodation, from wooden cabins to camping and hammocks. It is near Buff Bay, 19 miles (30km) west of Port Antonio.
Open: daily 09.00–18.00hrs.

◆
MOORE TOWN
This little village is the capital of the Windward Maroons. It is a difficult drive, along a steep, winding road 10 miles (16km) south of Port Antonio into the John Crow Mountains – but worth it to see the splendid, untamed landscapes.
In Moore Town is Bump Grave (near the school), with a monument to show this is where the Right Excellent Nanny (warrior Queen of the Maroons) is buried.

◆◆
NONSUCH CAVES AND ATHENRY GARDENS
Set high in the hills above the coast, about three miles (5km) southeast of Port Antonio, past lush thickets of jungle, slopes carpeted with ferns and dappled with dark-green trees, the caves lie in 185 acres (75 hectares) of working copra (coconut) plantation. You wander through pretty, well-kept gardens, with labelled plants, to the entrance of the caves (discovered in 1955 by a goat). They are reckoned to be over a million years old, and were thrust up from the bed of the sea. The blow holes in the roof of the caverns were caused by swirling water – bats cluster in them now – and you can see fossilised coral and stalagmite formations, including the 'pipe

Unspoilt beauty at Reach Falls

organ' that sounds different notes when hit.
The biggest cavern, called the 'cathedral room' is 40 feet (12m) high. From the viewing platform outside there are sweeping panoramas.
Open: daily 09.00 to 17.00hrs (the tour takes 1½hrs).

◆◆
REACH FALLS
After the tiny fishing village of Manchioneal, on the east coast, and just before the Drivers River bridge, a rough, winding track leads towards the mountains inland along a deep, forested valley. It is a remote spot, and these captivating waterfalls are completely unspoilt and secluded. There is, however, a small wooden booth where a couple of guides sit and you will be expected to give a tip afterwards. You walk down some narrow steps carved into the cliff beside the falls, into the

gorge where water plunges over rocks into a pool overhung by foliage – you can take a dip, and find the cave behind the falls. Reach Falls are about two miles (3km) from Manchioneal, which is 21 miles (33km) southeast of Port Antonio.
Open: daily 09.00 to 17.00hrs.

◆◆◆
RIO GRANDE RAFTING ✓

It was Errol Flynn who is said to have started organising races between the bamboo rafts that were used to transport bananas down river. This is the longest of the rafting trips: for two and a half hours you can sit back and tranquilly soak up some spectacular scenery (and a rum punch or beer), while the captain stands at the front of the raft skilfully navigating you down six miles (10km) of river. It starts high in the hills behind

Somerset Falls

Port Antonio, and follows a course which takes you to the coast.

The river is bordered by steep slopes, where the extravagant foliage is spangled with flowers, and exotic birds can be heard in the trees. In places there are sheer rocks each side, with curtains of greenery – you pass through a mossy stone archway called Lovers Lane, where you make a wish. You will also see charming vignettes such as children playing in the water or men fishing. There are stopping points with craft, drink or snack stands, and you can take an invigorating swim in the river. The trip ends at Rafters Rest, on the coast, where there is a bar, restaurant and souvenir shops. There are changing facilities at both ends of the trip, but if you are wearing swimwear take clothes to protect yourself from the hot sun. Official drivers will take your car down to Rafter's Rest (for an extra charge). They offer moonlight raft trips by arrangement. The starting point at Berridale is about six miles (10km) south of Port Antonio. Rafts run daily, starting 08.30 to 16.30hrs.

◆◆◆
SAM STREET'S AFRICAN ART MUSEUM

In the hills inland of Long Bay, on the east coast, in a house that used to be part of a rum factory, Dr Sam Street has a varied and personal collection of African art. It is definitely worth seeing. It lies about 15 miles (24km) southeast of Port Antonio. You'll have to take pot luck with opening hours.

Kingston, the heart of Jamaica

◆◆
SOMERSET FALLS

Near the coast, the Daniels River tumbles down a rocky gorge in a picturesque series of waterfalls, surrounded by steamy jungle. You can take a gondola trip along the river to see hidden falls and caves, swim in the green pools or picnic in peaceful gardens. It lies about two miles (3km) west of Port Antonio.

Open: daily 10.00–17.00hrs.

THE SOUTHEAST

This area covers the parishes of St Thomas, St Andrew and St Catherine, which are in the southern part of the counties of Surrey and Middlesex. The main attraction here is the capital city of Kingston, with its wealth of Jamaican culture – and nearby Port Royal, once notorious as the 'wicked' town of the buccaneers. There is also historic interest in the old capital of Spanish Town. But you will not find busy tourist resorts or a choice of fine beaches in this area.

The scenery in this part of the island is generally quite different to the north – especially on the dry, dusty coastal plains. There are typical savannah landscapes of golden grass wafting in the breeze, scattered with gnarled trees, spiky cacti and a few palms. The plains rise to rocky hillsides covered in bush and scrub vegetation. It only starts to look vividly green high up in the hills, and around river valleys or patches of swampland on the coast. Just a few miles inland of the parched coastal strip, the cool slopes of the Blue Mountains are clad in green foliage, pines and coffee plantations. The soaring, cloud-capped peaks provide a spectacular backdrop to Kingston and the coast. The main road east of Kingston hugs the coastline, which is dotted with little fishing villages. It skirts round the southeast tip of the island, Morant Point – with its lighthouse, made in London 150 years ago. Nearby in Holland

Bay there is a remote but very appealing beach.

West of Kingston, the main road heads inland, where the coastal plain is mostly much wider than along the north of the island. Apart from the backbone of central highlands inland, the two large promontories also have outcrops of scrubby hills – such as the bulge of the Hellshire Hills southwest of Kingston (where there are a couple of good beaches on the coast). Further west, the coast can only be reached by road in a few places. Extensive sugar cane plantations lie on the plains near Morant Point and west of Kingston. There are also some coconut and banana groves situated by the coast in the east, and towards the west, further inland, there are many citrus groves.

WHAT TO SEE

KINGSTON

Kingston is where the real, pulsating heart of Jamaica beats. The culture and commerce of the island are centred here as well as many of its people. What the city lacks in aesthetic appeal, its splendid setting more than makes up for. It sits beside a very impressive harbour – the world's seventh largest natural harbour. The Palisadoes Peninsula is a long thin spit of land that curves around it to the south, where the Norman Manley International Airport lies and at the western tip, Port Royal. From here you can appreciate magnificent views of the mountains rising behind the city. Apart from the cultural and

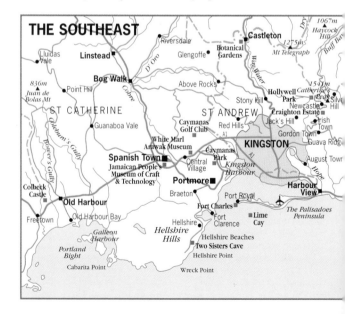

historic interest to be found in Kingston and its environs, you can also quickly leave the noise and dust behind by driving up into the Blue Mountains, a haven of beauty and tranquillity. Kingston was founded in the 17th century; and after Port Royal was devastated by an earthquake in 1692, survivors flocked to Kingston. In 1872 it became the new capital of Jamaica, and the seat of government was transferred from Spanish Town. In 1907, an earthquake and fire destroyed many of the old downtown buildings. During the last 30 years, there have been major attempts at reconstruction and revitalisation. But as the population continues to swell, the city exuberantly defies these efforts to discipline and order it. Kingston is a chaotic, crowded,

melting-pot of a city, and a mishmash of different architectural styles, from distinguished old colonial buildings to modern high-rise concrete blocks, and, in sharp contrast, the graffiti-daubed, scruffy tin and wood shacks of the ghetto areas in the west. The up-market residential suburbs tend to lie in the foothills, such as Beverley Hills to the east. Numerous bars, shops and a surprising number of churches line the busy, dusty central streets; reggae throbs from many corners; there are stalls and 'higglers' selling their wares from the pavement. And in places there are even goats or pigs snuffling around. Although Kingston is less dangerous than, say, New York or Miami, it is wise to avoid certain areas like

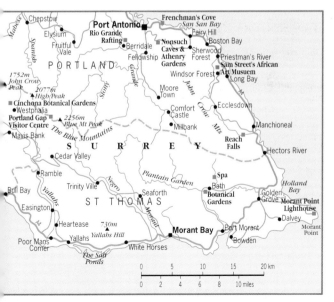

Trench Town. There is, of course, some crime – found in any big city – but Kingston also has vitality, excitement, sophistication and all sorts of entertainment.

The **downtown** area of Kingston, or city centre, actually lies around the waterfront in the south. This was the heart of the old city; but a recent facelift has given the broad boulevards many sparkling modern buildings including a conference centre, hotels, banks, offices and shops. From Pier 1 on the harbour, little water taxis leave for Port Royal. One of the attractions of the waterfront is the **Crafts Market,** in a big building in front of the piers, where you will find an excellent collection of local handicrafts. A few blocks east on Orange Street is the National Gallery of Art (see page 73). On the waterfront nearby, the big modern Bank of Jamaica has a **Coin and Note Museum.**

Further north, Orange Street is lined with colourful street stalls. In Duke Street, opposite Gordon House – where Jamaica's Parliament meets – and near the island's only synagogue, is **Headquarters House.** This fine 18th-century building, with white columns, was formerly the seat of government and the military. Nearby is **The Parade,** a spacious green square surrounded by wide boulevards, which was once the centre of Kingston. On one side is **Kingston Parish Church,** reconstructed in 1909 on original 17th-century foundations. The English

Admiral John Benbow is buried in the grounds – he died in 1702 after a battle with the French. The Parade is also bordered on its northern side by **Ward Theatre,** an attractive pale blue and white building dating from 1911, which hosts many good productions, not least the annual Pantomime. Further north is the 74-acre (30-hectare) **National Heroes Park,** with modern monuments dedicated to heroes such as Paul Bogle, as well as the tombs of Marcus Garvey and Norman Manley.

The **uptown** area includes New Kingston, a modern development of hotels, banks, shops and offices – including the Jamaica Tourist Board office on St Lucia Avenue. West of here is Half Way Tree, a main intersection in the city – where market people coming down from the mountains used to rest on the roots of a huge cottonwood tree. Close to the Half Way Tree intersection is **St Andrew's Parish Church,** which has the island's oldest church registers, dating back to 1666. Northeast of here, on Montrose Road, is **Vale Royal,** a splendid white 17th-century building which is the Prime Minister's residence; the lookout tower on the roof was used to watch movements of ships in the harbour.

There are several worthwhile sights to be visited in the uptown area – such as picturesque Devon House (see page 74). On Hope Road are the extensive and prettily landscaped grounds surrounding **Kings House,** the official residence of the governor-general – open to the

Nightlife dazzles in Kingston

public on weekdays. Further east is the **University of the West Indies** which sits on the site of the Old Mona and Papine sugar estates, and the ruins of the aqueduct and sugar factory are scattered over the campus. The Mona Campus Chapel, near the main gate, was originally an old sugar warehouse – built of stone in 1799 – which has been moved and faithfully reassembled here. By the university campus is the Papine Market, which bustles with life from Thursday to Saturday.

What to See Downtown

◆
AFRICAN CARIBBEAN INSTITUTE
12 Ocean Boulevard
Research into African traditions in Jamaica and the Caribbean is conducted here, and there is a display of arts and crafts; the library includes collections relating to the social and ethnic history of the island.
Open: Monday to Friday 09.00–16.00hrs.

◆◆
INSTITUTE OF JAMAICA
12 East Street
This was founded in the 19th century for the 'encouragement of literature, science and art'. It has the world's largest collection of reference material on the West Indies in the National Library of Jamaica, including some especially noteworthy lithographic prints of Jamaica and the Americas. Among the documents are the Shark Papers: a ship's log showing evidence of illicit trading which was tossed overboard when the boat was stopped by a British vessel in 1799, and later recovered in the stomach of a shark, leading to the guilty captain's conviction.
The complex includes the Natural History Division. There is a small museum, and the Institute hosts exhibitions, lectures and art shows.
Open: Monday to Thursday 08.30–17.00hrs.

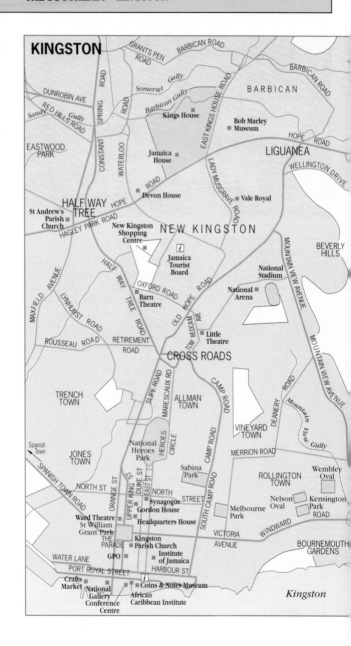

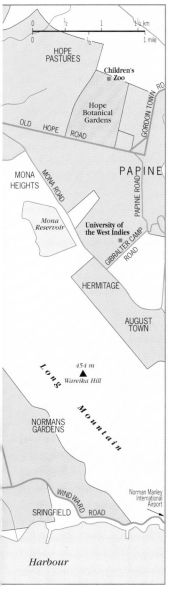

◆◆◆
NATIONAL GALLERY OF ART
Roy West Building, on the corner of Orange Street and Ocean Boulevard
An outstanding collection of Jamaican art is housed here, which goes back to colonial times – and includes an exciting display of works from this century. There are sculptures by Edna Manley (wife of Jamaica's second Prime Minister, and mother of another, Michael Manley), including the beautiful *Negro Aroused* (1939). One room is packed with the paintings and sculpture of leading artist Kapo (Mallica Reynolds). The gallery also contains a controversial big bronze statue of Bob Marley.
Open: Monday to Friday 11.00–16.30hrs.

What to See Uptown

◆◆
BOB MARLEY MUSEUM
56 Hope Road
You cannot miss the 19th-century mansion, with its Ethiopian flag and statue of Marley outside. The home and Tuff Gong recording studio of Jamaica's legendary reggae star is now a museum. Memorabilia and artwork show Marley's life from his childhood in the ghetto, to his years as a world-famous musician, and then early death from cancer.
Open: Monday, Tuesday, Thursday and Friday 09.00–17.30hrs; Wednesday and Saturday noon–18.00hrs.

♦♦♦
DEVON HOUSE
26 Hope Road, at the intersection of Waterloo Road
This elegant classical-style mansion was built in 1881 by one of the first black millionaires in the Caribbean – George Stiebel, who made his money mining gold in Venezuela. The inspiration for the design of the house came from buildings he admired in Venezuela. The house has been beautifully restored and furnished with period antiques in various historic styles of Jamaica – proudly showing off the deep, warm glow of much polished mahogany. Outside, butterflies flit among the flowers in its graceful gardens.
Open: Tuesday to Saturday, 10.00–17.00hrs.
The mellow brick stable blocks at the back have been turned into shops, selling a fine collection of Jamaican crafts; there is also a tempting cake shop and ice-cream parlour. They surround a picturesque garden courtyard where you can sit under a shady tree, or relax on the Coffee Terrace, with its cool tiles and 'gingerbread' fretwork. It also has two restaurants.
Open: Monday to Saturday; restaurants every day.

♦♦
HOPE BOTANICAL GARDENS
Old Hope Road, just north of the University
These are the largest botanical gardens in the West Indies. They were laid out in 1881 and cover 200 acres (81 hectares), resplendent with many exotic and colourful plants – there are spacious lawns, ornamental gardens and an Orchid House. The grounds also have a small zoo and amusement park.
Open: daily 08.30–18.30hrs.

Accommodation
Kingston's accommodation ranges from large hotels, which cater well for business travellers, to small guest houses.

Elegant Devon House

Some of the most appealing places lie outside the city. (There is also camping near the northwestern outskirts.) Unlike the rest of the island, where hotels have lower off-season rates, most Kingston hotels charge one rate all year. Among the higher-priced establishments is the modern high-rise **Jamaica Pegasus**, 81 Knutsford Boulevard (tel: 926 3690), in New Kingston; it is sophisticated but impersonal, with an excellent range of facilities including a pool and good shops. The **Wyndham New Kingston** 77 Knutsford Boulevard (tel: 926 5430), is another big tower; smart and spacious, it has a similar approach to the Pegasus, also with a wide range of facilities including a pool. The moderately-priced **Terra Nova Hotel**, 17 Waterloo Road (tel: 926 2211), lies just north of New Kingston past Devon House, in a colonial mansion surrounded by tropical gardens; it is quite small and quietly elegant, with a pool and popular restaurant.

Hotels at very reasonable or budget rates include the **Mayfair**, 4 West Kings House Close (tel: 926 1610), by the grounds of Kings House; it is quite small, with rooms in several separate houses – the lavish poolside buffet and barbecue (on Wednesday and Saturday) are firm favourites. In northern New Kingston is **The Courtleigh**, 31 Trafalgar Road (tel: 926 8174), with a well-kept, civilised atmosphere; it has a pool and disco, and also offers self-catering apartments. The

Island Club Resorts, 1 Hopedale Avenue (tel: 978 3915), is a small, comfortable, family-run hotel set on the slopes of Beverly Hills to the east; it has a pool and splendid views. On the northeastern outskirts, the **Ivor Guest House**, Jacks Hill (tel: 977 0033), has three rooms in a traditional wooden house with superb views. On the northwestern outskirts is the **Jonraine Country Inn**, 7 West Kirkland Heights, Red Hills (tel: 944 3513), small and personal with fine views. South of Kingston, by Port Royal (and near the airport), is the attractive, moderately-priced **Morgan's Harbour Hotel** (tel: 924 8464), set in gardens beside the harbour, with magnificent views across to Kingston and the mountains (the city can be quickly reached by its courtesy boat). It has a marina, a small beach, a pool, and a good range of watersports (including a diving club) and other facilities.

High in the Blue Mountains you can find secluded havens of tranquillity and yet more glorious panoramas. Nestling on the verdant slopes by Irish Town, about 10 miles (16km) northeast of central Kingston, lies the idyllic **Strawberry Hill** (tel: 944 8400). It has several enchanting villas individually designed in plantation-house style, with whitewashed wood, shingle roofs and spacious verandas; inside they are furnished with exquisite taste to echo the colonial era (but with every modern comfort). Some have kitchens, but there is also a restaurant; needless to say, this is a very expensive slice of heaven. At the other end of the price scale, about 16 miles (26km) from Kingston, in the midst of a coffee plantation just north of Guava Ridge is the little **Pine Grove Hotel** (tel: 922 8705; postal address: 62 Duke Street, Kingston); it has simple rooms and cottages with cooking facilities, or you can eat in the dining room.

Also at budget prices, **Paraiso** (tel: 977 8007) is a gracious house set in gardens and farmland at Guava Ridge, offering bed and breakfast in two rooms.

Nightlife and Entertainment

There are several companies offering organised trips all over the island (such as JUTA, 85 Knutsford Boulevard) – the Tourist Board or hotels can give you information. If you want to take a boat ride across the harbour, catch the little ferry from the pier near the Crafts Market to Port Royal; there are regular departures through the day, with more on Saturdays and fewer on Sundays. Alternatively, small boats leave the ferry jetty at the Fishermen's Beach in Port Royal for Lime Cay (see page 80).

Kingston's humming heartbeat continues well into the night, with a variety of nightclubs, discos and bars. Some of the hotels have popular nightspots. For instance, the **Jonkanoo Lounge** at the Wyndham Hotel, is a posh place that has slick nightclub acts, and dancing for the 'mature' crowd. The Jamaica Pegasus Hotel also has various

evening entertainments. The Courtleigh hotel has a lively disco, **Mingles**. (For addresses, see above under **Accommodation**.)

Popular discos and nightclubs include: the **Mirage**, Sovereign Centre, Hope Road, with its state-of-the-art design; **Peppers**, 31 Upper Waterloo Road; **Godfathers**, 69 Knutsford Boulevard; **Chasers**, 29 Barbican Road; **Grizzly's**, 6A Holborn Road; and the **Countryside Club**, 19 Eastwood Park Road. At Devon House, the **Grog Shoppe** offers exotic rum cocktails and dancing under the stars.

If you are interested in live music, contact the Tourist Board, ask your hotel or consult listings in *The Daily Gleaner*. The **National Stadium**, the **Ranny Williams Performance Centre** and the University's **Creative Arts Centre** occasionally put on shows; and entertainment, including reggae, is frequently held at the **centre** by Fort Clarence Beach.

The **Skateland Rolla Disco,** 7½ Constant Spring Road has a huge rink, and a live band on Wednesday nights.

Theatres

Kingston is the centre of Jamaica's cultural entertainments, and theatres boast a wide variety of shows and concerts. The **Ward Theatre,** North Parade, has excellent dramatic and musical performances. The **National Pantomime** is a Jamaican institution, held here from Boxing Day to April, offering song and dance, satirical commentaries on current affairs, witty spoofs of historic events – and plenty of audience reaction. The **Little Theatre**, 4 Tom Redcam Avenue, hosts plays, dance and folk concerts. This is where you can see the brilliant **National Dance Theatre Company** perform innovative dances that draw inspiration from the kaleidoscope of ethnic influences on the island – the absolute acme of Jamaican grace and rhythm. The main season is from mid-July to mid-August, but there is a short series of performances at the end of November and beginning of December. This theatre also hosts an annual season of concerts by Olive Lewin's **Jamaican Folk Singers**, who combine movement with music to provide entertainment that is educational.

The **Barn Theatre**, 5 Oxford Road, is the island's most highly acclaimed theatre company. Consult the Tourist Board, your hotel or *The Daily Gleaner* for details of classical concerts and other musical events. The University's Creative Arts Centre holds concerts and cultural shows.

Restaurants

Kingston boasts a wide choice of places to eat, ranging from those offering a gourmet menu and sophisticated ambience to Chinese restaurants and burger bars. Many of the hotels are worth trying, including those mentioned above. The stunning views over the city make the **Ivor Guest House** (tel: 977 0033) an ideal place for lunch or early evening cocktail.

The Ward Theatre

One of Kingston's most renowned restaurants is the **Blue Mountain Inn**, on the Gordon Town road (tel: 927 1700). This 18th-century, colonial coffee plantation house is secluded in a deep valley beside the Hope River. The mountain setting is spectacular and there are terraces overlooking lush gardens. It opens for dinner only, and is expensive (the wine list is good) – but the surroundings make it special.

At Devon House you have a choice of restaurants: the **Devonshire** (tel: 929 7046), the most sophisticated, overlooking the garden courtyard; the informal, inexpensive **Grog Shoppe** (tel: 929 7027) set on the patio and specialising in Jamaican dishes; or the **Coffee**

Terrace (tel: 929 7063) which is good for breakfast or tea, but is not open in the evening like the other two.

If you're after *ital* food (vegetarian Rasta food), try **Minnie's Ethiopian Herbal Health Food Restaurant,** 176 Old Hope Road (tel: 927 9207). Minnie used to cook for Bob Marley, and you can sample some tasty, often piquant, vegetarian fare; the Friday night live reggae adds an authentic flavour.

Morgan's Harbour Hotel (tel: 924 8464) offers great seafood. For an excellent fish lunch at lower prices, but with similarly wonderful views across the harbour, try the **Fisherman's Cabin** (no phone) at Port Royal by the Fisherman's Beach – where pelicans can often be seen diving for their own lunch. If you fancy a finger-licking-good snack of freshly caught and fried fish, served with festival (crispy fried dumpling) or bammy (fried cassava bread), visit one of the beachside shacks at Hellshire Beach.

Shopping

As you would expect in a capital city, the opportunities for shopping are excellent, and for bargains, too. The **Crafts Market**, by the waterfront on Port Royal Street has the island's largest collection of local crafts – myriad arrays of handmade straw and woven goods, wood carvings, embroidery and more unusual items like dried calabashes or yoyos made from cacoon (a large seed from a vine pod). The market is located within a large building, but there are also lots of pavement higglers outside. Craft souvenirs may be cheaper here than in the north coast resorts, as higglers often buy goods in Kingston and sell them elsewhere on the island. If you enjoy visiting markets, you can find a variety of everyday items at the bustling **Coronation Market,** on Lower Spanish Town Road, or **Papine Market** by the university campus (both in action at the end of the week).

The pretty little shops behind **Devon House**, 26 Hope Road, where you can browse without being hassled, offer a good selection of fine crafts and interesting gifts, including pottery, leather goods, carving, dolls and baskets.

There are several modern shopping plazas in Kingston, such as the **New Kingston Shopping Centre**, 30 Dominica Drive, which has over 30 shops housed in a smart complex around a courtyard with a splashing fountain and a large, free underground car park; there are some stylish shops here. Another shopping complex worth visiting is **The**

Springs, Half Way Tree Road, which has designer boutiques and a good bookshop. Other plazas include the **Sovereign Centre**, 106 Hope Road, and the **Manor Shopping Centre**, Constant Spring Road. There are several shops selling duty-free items around Kingston, such as in the **Mall Plaza**, 20 Constant Spring Road; the **Jamaica Pegasus Hotel** on Knutsford Boulevard also has a duty-free shop.

For quality Jamaican art try **Contemporary Art Centre**, 1 Liguanea Avenue; the **Frame Centre Gallery**, 10 Tangerine Place; **Four Corners Gallery**, 7 West Arcadia Avenue; **Grosvenor Galleries**, 1 Grosvenor Terrace; **The Artisan**, 14 Dominica Drive; **Babylon Jamaica**, 10A West Kings House Road; **Chelsea Gallery**, 6 St Lucia Avenue; and **Bolivar Gallery** (which also has a bookshop) located at the corner of Half Way Tree and Grove roads.

If you are looking out for reggae records, try one of the music shops (and stalls) in Orange Street or on The Parade, as well as the shopping plazas.

Sports

Active visitors will find enough to keep them on their toes in Kingston, and spectators can also enjoy a variety of sports. Watersports are centred on **Morgan's Harbour Hotel** and Marina. From here you can go diving to explore the sunken remains of Port Royal, or snorkelling to see the colourful coral and tropical fishes. Otherwise there are opportunities for waterskiing, windsurfing, sailing and deep-sea fishing. You can also contact the **Royal Jamaica Yacht Club**, further east along the Palisadoes peninsula beside the harbour, if you wish to charter a boat. Morgan's Harbour Hotel offers other sports, including horse-riding.

Golf enthusiasts can find two championship courses in the area: the **Caymanas Golf Club**, lying 10 miles (16km) west of central Kingston, has a challenging course; **Constant Spring Golf Club** is set on a hillside north of the city with splendid views (it also has tennis, badminton and squash

Traditional costumes in the New Kingston Shopping Centre

courts, and a pool). Major golf tournaments are held at both of these clubs.

You can watch various equestrian events at **Caymanas Park**, where polo is played every Thursday and Sunday; you can also have a flutter on the horse-racing at Caymanas Park, on Wednesdays, Saturdays or holidays. Other spectator sports include cricket at Sabina Park, from January to August.

Events
The capital hosts a multitude of different events through the year. One which draws crowds from around the world, to hear reggae performed by top artists, is the **Reggae SunSplash**, in July/August. You can also hear live reggae, as well as soca and pop, at the big **Superjam** festival in late December.

The University of the West Indies has a carnival in February, while the **Jamaica Carnival** and **Orange Carnival** both take place in April. There are events, shows and competitions of every description during **Festival!** in July, leading up to the celebrations for **Independence Day** on the first Monday in August, which include a street parade and grand gala.

Oktoberfest is a festival with a German theme, in October. Flower-lovers can enjoy shows put on by the **Jamaica Orchid Society which are held** at the end of March and beginning of October. The **St Elizabeth Horticultural Society Flower Show** in late April is the largest in the Caribbean.

Contact the Tourist Board for information on events.

Beaches
Lying offshore, south of Kingston Harbour, is **Lime Cay** – a pretty coral islet with a pale sandy beach, ideal for swimming, snorkelling or picnicking. It can be reached by a small boat from Morgan's Harbour Hotel or the Fisherman's Beach, Port Royal. Other beaches to try are on the Hellshire coast southwest of the city. **Fort Clarence** is a sandy beach with changing facilities. A little further down the coast is **Hellshire Beach**, a fine stretch of sand very popular with locals. At the back of the beach are bamboo shacks where women

Hot stuff: Jamaican limbo

fry fresh fish and bammy – the wafting aromas are quite irresistible.

There are two other sandy beaches in the southeast area that are worth a visit if you are passing; both are very remote and unspoilt. **Holland Bay** is a white-sand beach bordered by cliffs which lies along the little road to Morant Point Lighthouse, on the southeastern tip of the island, about 48 miles (76km) east of Kingston. Near the fishing hamlet of Rocky Point is **Jackson Bay**, about 48 miles (76km) southwest of Kingston.

WHAT ELSE TO SEE IN THE SOUTHEAST

◆
BATH

There is little to show that this was a fashionable watering place in the 18th century, as it is now just a small, quiet farming community, although the reputed therapeutic value of the hot springs continues to attract visitors. The springs were discovered 300 years ago, after a runaway slave claimed that bathing in the waters had cured chronic ulcers on his legs. The **Bath Fountain** mineral spa was originally opened in 1747, and lies just outside the town. The water emerges from the rocks at two different temperatures, which is mixed to give hot baths; the high lime and sulphur content is regarded as beneficial for treating rheumatic ailments and skin diseases. There are plans to renovate the simple spa building and hotel this year.
Open: daily.

In the centre of town are the **Botanical Gardens**, the only other evidence of Bath's distinguished past – they were established in 1779. Hurricane Gilbert caused extensive damage here in 1988, although the gardens have since undergone some restoration. In one corner are the offspring of the original breadfruit brought from Tahiti by Captain Bligh of the *Bounty*.
Open: daily 08.00–16.00hrs.

THE BLUE MOUNTAINS ✓

This ridge of magnificent peaks dominates the eastern end of the island; many soar over 6,000 feet (1,829m), and the rounded Blue Mountain Peak reaches 7,402 feet (2,256m) – the highest point on the island. The cool climate here averages 65°F (18°C) during the day. The upper reaches are often swathed in swirling mist by mid-morning, which gives them a hazy blue cast from a distance.

Whichever way you approach the mountains, the route will be tortuous and often rough – and to get to the summit involves a long, strenuous hike up a steep track. The southern slopes are more accessible than those on the Portland side of the ridge, to the north – where torrential rainfall has deterred people from clearing the rugged terrain of its densely tangled tropical forests in order to settle and use the land, as has happened in parts of the south side, especially the area close to Kingston. The landscapes and panoramas are inspirational.

Gordon Town lies 1,200 feet (366m) up in the Hope River valley, a few miles northeast of Kingston, and nestles in a profusion of colourful plants. Many of the plants found here are descendants of those imported for a long-vanished botanical garden, but which have remained an important part of the island flora of Jamaica – such as hibiscus, oleander, jasmine, azalea, magnolia and cassia. The winding road climbs the mountain sides, heading east towards **Guava Ridge**. Many of the houses here are surrounded by patches of vegetables and fruit, from yams to asparagus, banana palms to strawberry plants. This is where most of Kingston's fresh produce comes from: towards the end of the week, the smallholders head towards the city to sell their wares in one of the markets. This way of life has hardly changed in 150 years, since the emancipated slaves originally settled on this free land. Further along you pass **'World's End'**, a distillery run by the Scot Ian Sangster; you can tour the factory and taste the rum and liqueurs produced under the 'Sangster's Old Jamaica' label.

Going north from Guava Ridge, a few miles past the Pine Grove Hotel, is the riverside forestry station of **Clydesdale**. It used to be a coffee plantation – you can still see an old waterwheel and coffee-drying barbecues – but now there are stretches of

young conifer trees. Nearby is the **Cinchona Botanical Gardens**, in a stunning setting high on a mountain ridge that drops steeply from 5,500 to 4,500 feet (1,670 to 1,370m) with three river valleys far below. It was originally established as a cinchona and Assam tea plantation in 1868 – cinchona is a tree from whose bark quinine is obtained – but in the face of large-scale competition from India, it failed.

This region produces coffee that is renowned for its flavour throughout the world. Several old plantation Great Houses remain, mostly built during the boom period of the early 19th century – the coffee plantations themselves have declined since then. To the northwest of Cinchona is **Silver Hill,** with one of the Blue Mountains' few coffee factories (another is near Mavis Bank; visitors are welcome at both factories). West of Silver Hill lies **Hollywell Park**, where the mountain slopes around Hardwar Gap are covered in a 300-acre (120-hectare) forest reserve. Thatched rondavels offer shelter for picnickers, necessary as it is a misty area with heavy rainfall – but the peaceful surroundings and vistas of Kingston are splendid. It is a great place for hiking, with miles of trails.

Just a couple of miles (3km) southeast is **Newcastle,** 18 miles (29km) northeast of Kingston, a training camp for the Jamaica Defence Force set on a mountainside, at approximately 4,000 feet (1,219m) overlooking the Mammee River valley.

Blue Mountain Peak

It was established in 1841 as a hill station for the British troops, at a time when diseases like yellow fever took a fatal toll at low altitudes. South of here is **Irish Town**, where tours can be taken around the coffee plantation and fine old Great House of the nearby **Craighton Estate**.

You have to be determined and fit to make it to the top of the **Blue Mountain Peak**. From Mavis Bank, 16 miles (26km) east of Kingston, it is a tough climb up a rough track, which takes at least three hours. The route takes you through thick forest until, at around 5,500 feet (1,676m), open woodland takes over. The peaks are often cloaked in mist from mid-morning to around 18.00hrs, which gives the scenery a rather other-worldly look. The spectacular isolation, and breathtaking panoramas over the whole island make the climb worthwhile. On a clear day, Cuba can be seen in the distance to the north. The classic hike starts at 02.00 or 03.00hrs to reach the peak in time for a sensational sunrise. A practical point: climbers need strong, comfortable shoes and warm clothes. The magic of the Blue Mountains is better appreciated if you give yourself two days to explore, and stay overnight (or longer). There is a variety of accommodation available in the area – mostly quite simple. The Tourist Board provides information. Otherwise, for details of cabins, rooms, camping and hikes (guided or on your own, from half-a-day to five-day backpacking treks), contact Peter Bentley, Maya Lodge, PO Box 216, Kingston 7 (tel: 927 2097). This includes information on cabins or camping at Clydesdale and Hollywell, but for log cabins here you can also contact the Forestry Department, 173 Constant Spring Road, Kingston (tel: 924 2667). The Jamaica Defence Force has cottages to rent at Cinchona and Newcastle – details from Newcastle Hill Sta 1T (tel: 944 8230). The classy Strawberry Hill, the Pine Grove Hotel and Paraiso Bed and Breakfast are described under Kingston's **Accommodation** (see pages 74–6). Whitfield Hall is a hostel in an old coffee plantation house, set at 4,200 feet (1,280m) not far from the Blue Mountain Peak. There is also a simple cottage with cooking facilities on the summit.

◆
MORANT BAY

This tiny, quiet town on the south coast, 32 miles (51km) east of Kingston, is of interest because this is where the slaves' Morant Bay Rebellion took place in 1865. A statue of Paul Bogle, the Baptist preacher who led the rebellion, stands in the town square by the courthouse. The statue was created by Edna Manley, the Jamaican sculptor. Morant Bay's original courthouse burnt down during the rebellion, and Bogle was hanged inside the gutted shell.

◆
OLD HARBOUR

Lying on the coastal plain, not far from the sea, about 24 miles (38km) west of Kingston, this is a typical local town – with a Victorian clock tower near the

centre. Just northwest of the town lie the ruins of Colbeck Castle. This fortified stone mansion, with slave quarters underground, is thought to have been built in the 17th century by an unpopular Englishman, Colonel John Colbeck (who served under Cromwell).

◆◆◆
PORT ROYAL

The quiet atmosphere of this fishing village, at the entrance to Kingston Harbour, belies its glittering (if dissolute) past. In the 17th century it became the infamous lair of the swashbuckling buccaneers, who squandered their ill-gotten loot on wine (or rum), and wild times. Port Royal was also important in the 18th century as the regional headquarters of the British Royal Navy. Recognising its strategic importance, the English built a fort here within a year of their capture of Jamaica in 1655. Port Royal gained its name in 1662, at the time of the Restoration in England; and the fort was christened Fort Charles, in honour of King Charles II. A settlement quickly sprung up around the fort; although the site was poor for the development of a town, it had the great advantages of a magnificent harbour and deep anchorage alongside. It became a base for trade and the buccaneers' attacks on Spanish ships and ports (at first encouraged by the English) – which brought increasing riches to Port Royal. In Port Royal's heyday, Spanish gold and silver were the coinage used here.

The town was ringed by six fortresses, and by 1688 was jam-packed with some 1,200 houses (most were four storeys high – with rents equally elevated); it had thousands of inhabitants. There was a proliferation of taverns and rum shops, which numbered one for every ten residents, as well as brothels, gaming houses and goldsmiths. The legendary reprobate and buccaneer, Henry Morgan, who even became governor of Jamaica, was very much at home here and this was where he was buried. Perhaps it was appropriate that the town should meet a violent and dramatic end, like many of its inhabitants. Certainly many believed it was divine retribution when an earthquake struck it down in 1692. About 2,000 lives were lost as buildings collapsed in clouds of dust and great fissures swallowed them. In a matter of minutes, two-thirds of Port Royal had plunged beneath the sea; devastation and chaos reigned amid the horrifying carnage.

Rebuilding started, trade was revived, but Port Royal suffered a series of further blows – first a fire reduced the town to ashes in 1704, then the following 47 years saw it hit by five ferocious hurricanes. Port Royal refused to die, but these disasters helped ensure that it never recovered the character of its former days of infamy and fortune. Kingston, across the harbour, replaced Port Royal as the island's chief trading centre.

During the 18th century, the Caribbean was the scene of continuous maritime conflict between the British, French and Spanish. Port Royal was increasingly used by the Royal Navy, and emerged as the most important British naval station in the Caribbean, until it literally went out in a blaze of glory, ravaged by a fire in 1815. The naval dockyard closed in 1905.

As you approach Port Royal today, you pass a long red-brick wall which enclosed the old naval dockyard – today Morgan's Harbour Hotel lies on the site. From here you can look across to the sinister saltmarsh of Gallows Point, where many pirates met their end. Among these was 'Calico Jack' Rackham; after being hung, his body was then

Passing time in Port Royal...

squeezed into an iron frame and strung up as a gruesome deterrent to others, on a sandy cay off Port Royal which still bears his name. The sunken city adds an intriguing dimension to this historic site – with legends of sunken treasure – and some claim to have heard the eerie tolling of underwater church bells on stormy days.

Towards the far end of Port Royal – and at some distance from its original position right on the sea – is **Fort Charles**. This is one of the oldest and best-reserved of Jamaica's many forts. It dates from 1656, although repairs and additions changed it considerably over the years. On one side you can see the raised wooden platform where Nelson (put in charge here for a short time at the age of 20) watched anxiously for a French invasion that never came – today called Nelson's Quarterdeck. The fort also has a **Maritime Museum**.

To the south is the **Victoria and Albert Battery**, a defensive structure built in 1888 along with the Royal Artillery Store at one end, which is better known as the Giddy House since it became tilted at a rakish angle in the 1907 earthquake. The origin of its nickname is obvious if you try walking inside. Just north of the parade ground is the long impressive **Old Naval Hospital**, built in 1819. The building is of interest as one of the earliest to be constructed of prefabricated cast-iron sections, brought out from England. It houses the **Museum of Historical Archaeology**, which has an interesting display of objects recovered from the sunken city – such as candelabra, bottles, silver, bone wig curlers and ivory articles.

Not far from the entrance breach in the old walls around Port Royal, lies **St Peter's Church**. This building dates from 1725, and inside there is a striking organ loft, erected in 1743, with palm-leaf carvings and elaborate mouldings. Some of the memorials give a good picture of life (or death) in the 18th and 19th centuries. In the churchyard lies the tomb of Louis Galdy who had an extraordinary escape in the earthquake when the ground opened to swallow him – and then spat him out again into the sea.

Nearby is the village itself, where little terraced houses with verandas line the small streets behind the Fisherman's Beach. There is a jetty here where the connecting ferry to Kingston arrives and boats go to Lime Cay.

Port Royal has other historic sites and buildings – such as the 19th-century military hospital beside the church and the old jail (parts of which probably predate the 1692 earthquake)

– so it is worth looking at a map which shows details of these. Fort Charles and other sights open daily, l0.00–16.00hrs. The small passenger ferry from Kingston runs several times throughout the day; otherwise it is about 14 miles (22km) from downtown Kingston by road. There are plans afoot for major redevelopment of the area, including a reconstruction of the 17th-century town of Port Royal and new museums.

◆◆◆
SPANISH TOWN
Founded by a son of Christopher Columbus, this was the capital of Jamaica for over 300 years. Most of the original Spanish buildings were destroyed by the English in a fit of pique, when they arrived in 1655 to find the town empty and bare of booty, the Spaniards having already fled with their valuables. It continued to be the colonial capital under the British – who gave it its present name – until 1872.

In the centre of this sizeable town is a serene and graceful **square** (The Park), first set out by the Spanish. The well-kept central garden is dominated by elegant royal palms, and bordered by splendid Georgian buildings. On one side sits the old British **House of Assembly**, dating from 1762 and now housing the local parish council offices. It is a red-brick building with a superb shady colonnade running along its length and a pillared wooden balcony above. Opposite lies **Old King's House** (also built in

1762) which was the residence of the island's governor; in 1925 it was gutted by fire, but the impressive façade with its grand portico remain to bear witness that this was considered the finest governor's residence in the British Colonies. The stable block houses the **Jamaican People's Museum of Craft and Technology**, a folk museum which has displays of cultural relics showing agricultural, industrial and architectural methods used in Jamaica – varying from home utensils to a carriage, a pimento fanner, and a village store.
Open: Monday to Friday l0.00–17.00hrs.

On the south side of the square, the large red-brick **Courthouse** (1819) suffered the same fate as King's House and was devastated by a fire several years ago. Opposite is a classically grand white-stucco structure, in the centre of which is the **Rodney Memorial**, honouring Admiral Rodney who saved the island from invasion by the French in 1782 (not in Roman times, as the statue's clothing suggests). There are some other graceful old buildings in the area around the square.

A few blocks south on Barrett Street is the **Cathedral of St Jago de la Vega** (also called the Cathedral Church of St James). The present building was erected in 1714, and it is the second oldest building on the island (after Fort Charles at Port Royal). It is an attractive brick church built in the form of a cross, set in tranquil walled gardens, the brick tower (added in 1831) is crowned by a white wood spire with a pointed red shingle roof. It contains several memorials to notable figures in Jamaican history.

Spanish Town lies about 14 miles (22km) west of downtown Kingston. Almost three miles (5km) east of Spanish Town, beside the main road to Kingston, is the **White Marl Arawak Museum** – on the site of the island's largest Arawak settlement. The design of the polygonal building was inspired by a *caneye*, a traditional Arawak Indian dwelling. Jamaica's main collection of Arawak artefacts is housed here. *Open*: Monday to Friday 10.00–16.00hrs.

Deep in the hills about 9 miles (14km) northwest of Spanish Town, just past Guanaboa Vale, is the **Mountain River Cave**. Ask a local to guide you along a rough path to this ancient cave which contains Arawak drawings. Mostly on flat limestone surfaces, there are designs of birds, turtles and hunters.

Spanish Town

THE SOUTHWEST

This area includes the parishes of Manchester and Clarendon, lying in the western part of the county of Middlesex, plus St Elizabeth and south Westmoreland, which lie in the county of Cornwall. Mandeville is the largest town, set in the cool highlands inland. There are no resorts aimed at mass tourism – though there are a few little places along the coast with small hotels or simple guest houses, such as Treasure Beach and Black River. It is the unspoilt, natural appeal of the area that gives it such great charm – and environmentalists are fighting to keep the developers at bay.

On the rolling, wooded hills around Mandeville, cattle graze in green pastures, while further north, the peaks and deep valleys of the mountain plateau are cloaked in jungle – such as along the spectacular southern edge of Cockpit Country. South of Mandeville, the high hills continue right down to the coast, where they are covered in bush and scrub, dotted with sabal thatch palms. The rocky ridge of the Santa Cruz

Blue skies at Black River

Mountains also runs to the coast near here. Much of the landscape looks parched in this area – especially around Treasure Beach, set in hot, still savannah grassland.

North of Treasure Beach, the Black River passes through verdant valleys to the flat wetlands and mangrove swamps on the coast – where there is a wealth of wildlife. The highlands sweep down to the coast again further northwest, and steep green slopes provide a picturesque backdrop to Bluefields Bay.

On the flat coastal plain around Savanna-la-Mar there are extensive sugar plantations, as well as inland in St Elizabeth; a profusion of citrus groves can be seen further east. Near Mandeville, the landscapes bear the rusty-red scars of open-cast bauxite mines.

In the traditional farming communities inland and fishing villages along the coast, the pattern of life is simple, languid and little changed for the last 100 years. The coast boasts some pretty beaches, which may lack the finesse of those along the north, but they are quite unspoilt and often deserted. From Treasure Beach eastwards the beaches are of dark sand, interspersed with rocky headlands and cliffs. The bays and coves west of Black River have pale, silvery sands. From this coast, the views of the sunsets are stunning.

This is not the swish Jamaica of the tourist brochures, but a haven for those who really want to get away from it all.

◆◆
BLACK RIVER

Sitting snugly on a big sheltered bay at the mouth of the Black River, this charming fishing town was Jamaica's second most important port (after Kingston) a century ago – when it became the first town on the island to have electricity. It was once a major exporter of logwood, a tree from which indigo dye was produced until synthetic means were found to manufacture it. Now its days of wealth and prominence as a port have long gone. There are many Georgian gingerbread-style houses, especially along the main sea-road going west out of the centre. Some of these wooden buildings obviously once had an elegant demeanour, but now they have entered a rickety and creaky old age – though the characteristic lacy fretwork still makes them extremely picturesque.

Around the centre, which lies beside the sea, are some old cream-painted clapboard houses, with overhanging upper storeys supported by columns over the street. On the high street is the local Tourist Board office. By the main road junction is St John's Parish Church, founded in 1837; one of the curates, who is buried here, was a distant relative of William Shakespeare. This quiet little town explodes with colour and activity on Friday and Saturday,

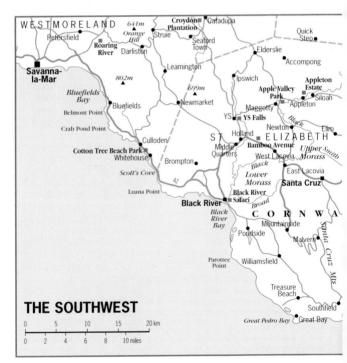

THE SOUTHWEST

| 0 | 5 | 10 | 15 | 20 km |

| 0 | 2 | 4 | 6 | 8 | 10 miles |

when the market takes place. The area around Black River is a splash of green in the dry savannah landscapes along the coast. Black River Safari boat trips (see page 98) explore the flat swamplands stretching inland – where there is some fascinating wildlife.

Just southeast lies Crane Beach, a narrow curve of creamy sand around the calm, peaceful bay.

Accommodation

Set beside the main seafront road is the attractive, comfortable **Invercauld Great House Hotel** (tel: 965 2750), a 100-year-old wooden 'gingerbread' house with decorative fretwork. Inside the airy white building, it is rather smart and the style is traditional; it has a good range of facilities, including a pool and disco, and prices would suit the budget-minded. Just along the road, the **Waterloo Guest House** (tel: 965 2278) is another 'gingerbread' house with much character (and a modern annexe); old-fashioned and quite basic, it has a homely appeal – and very low prices. Outside Black River, beside Crane Beach, lies the small, simple **Port of Call Hotel** (tel: 965 2360).

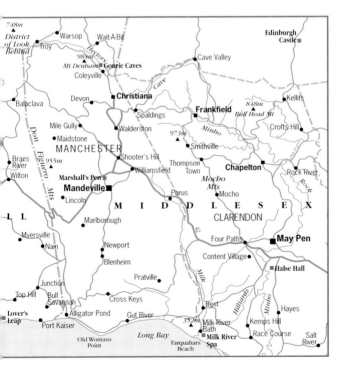

Budget accommodation can also be found several miles along the coast northwest of Black River. At Whitehouse is the **South Sea View Guest House** (tel: 965 2550), a modern villa set by the sea, with a pool and steps down to a rocky cove. Further up the coast at Culloden is **Natania's** (tel: 963 5342), an appealing, well-kept guesthouse; it has a pool and pretty gardens leading down to the rocky shoreline with a sunbathing area and jetty (watersports are available).

Restaurants

The **Invercauld Great House** has a pleasant restaurant, which is well worth trying. The **Waterloo Guest House** offers good-value home-style meals. **Natania's** has a good seafood restaurant. And the **South Sea View Guest House** serves tasty Jamaican dishes.

◆◆◆

MANDEVILLE

This calm, rather genteel town is cradled on the slopes inland at 2,000 feet (609m) where the clear mountain air and cooler temperatures used to attract British colonists on leave from hot, sticky Kingston. Mandeville was founded in 1814, when the parish was named after the Jamaican governor, the Duke of Manchester, and the town after his son, Lord Mandeville. And it soon became a playground for European gentry. When the British colonial days were over, and the holiday emphasis shifted to the beaches, Mandeville's popularity as a resort declined. But it is still a well-heeled and expanding town, largely thanks to the bauxite industry of the region, and also because it is the area's agricultural centre for fruit and vegetables.

The town is scattered over green hillsides, surrounded by pastures bounded by drystone walls and leafy woods. Well-kept and orderly, Mandeville boasts no slums. The centre lies around a square with a traditional green; beside it sit the Georgian **courthouse** and the **Parish Church**, both built in 1820 using limestone blocks which were cut by slaves. The busy market has stalls in front of the church.

A rickety reminder of Black River's past grandeur

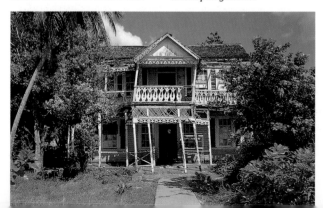

Among the many fine colonial houses around Mandeville, Marshall's Pen is outstanding (see page 100).

Another enjoyable visit is to **Mrs Stephenson's Garden.** The highlight is her array of orchids, in a myriad heavenly hues; she also grows shiny red anthuriums and citrus trees. Carmen Stephenson has won countless prizes for her flowers at the annual Horticultural Show in May (Manchester's Horticultural Society has been running for 130 years).

There are several factories north of town, to which tours can be arranged. These include **Pickapeppa Factory** at Shooter's Hill, where the popular piquant sauce is produced; the **High Mountain Coffee Factory** and the **Pioneer Chocolate Company**, both at Williamsfield. Trips can also be arranged to the local bammy factory, where traditional cassava bread is made.

Amid splendid mountain scenery to the north of Mandeville is the unspoilt, old-fashioned market town of **Christiana**, with crops like coffee and bananas growing on the slopes around it. Here you can visit the **Magic Toy Factory**, which makes distinctive wooden toys.

Arrangements to visit these sights and many others can be made through your hotel, or the information centre at the Astra Country Inn (see below). The Astra is run by Diana McIntyre-Pike, who has a wealth of information at her polished fingertips. She energetically promotes 'community tourism',

and is fighting to ensure the development of tourism in southern and central areas will not harm its natural character. She also organises Countrystyle holidays, personalised arrangements for guided tours or accommodation (or both), where visitors can get to know the countryside, the culture and the people – throughout Jamaica, but especially in the south.

Accommodation

There are two hotels in Mandeville run by the McIntyre clan, at budget rates. The small **Astra Country Inn** (tel: 962 3265) is quite simple and homely, with a friendly, personal atmosphere. It has some family rooms and suites with kitchenettes; facilities include a cosy pub (the Revival Room), a pool, and information centre. The comfortable **Mandeville Hotel** (tel: 962 2138), originally built as a hotel in 1875, is very traditional; it has suites with kitchens, a pool set in shady gardens, and sometimes has entertainment. Diana McIntyre-Pike also runs a bed and breakfast scheme in private homes and guest houses, which is very good value and includes places with much character. Set in the mountains just outside Christiana, about 15 miles (24km) north of Mandeville, is the small budget-priced **Hotel Villa Bella** (tel: 964 2243) in a plantation house surrounded by citrus and coffee trees. Furnished with simple good taste, it has an old-fashioned graciousness and charm – and glorious views.

Mandeville courthouse

specialises in health foods) and the **Mandeville Hotel**. The **Den**, Caledonia Road (tel: 962 3603), has a shady beer garden and serves delicious, reasonably-priced Jamaican dishes. If you want to go Chinese, try the **International**, Manchester Road (tel: 962 9527).

The **Nasterium** restaurant at the Hotel Villa Bella (see **Accommodation**), near Christiana, features Jamaican and Oriental cuisine, with wonderful views from the outdoor terrace (so it's a good spot for lunch or tea).

Nightlife and Entertainment

The Astra and Mandeville hotels can arrange all sorts of trips in the area and further afield. Walking and bird watching are popular here; Robert Sutton, at Marshall's Pen, is a leading Jamaican ornithologist, and he offers tours of the bird sanctuary at his family home, as well as Cockpit Country or the coast. Wildlife can also be seen on the **Black River Safari**.

Although Mandeville is a quiet town, it does have some action after dark. There are several discos and nightclubs to check out: **Sparks** (beside the Villa Shopping Centre), **Rock Steady** (at the Manchester Shopping Centre), **Tracks** (at the Mandeville Shopping Plaza), and **Planet** (Perth Road). The liveliest local nightclub is **Jim's HQ** at Gutters, about 10 miles (16km) to the southwest.

Restaurants

Traditional home cooking is on the menu at the **Astra Country Fresh** restaurant (which

Shopping

Mandeville has several modern shopping plazas; the main one is the **Manchester Shopping Centre**, Caledonia Road, where you will find **Craft Things Jamaican** selling local handicrafts. The **SWA Craft Centre** (7 North Crescent) is a community project to train girls who have just left school. They produce popular 'Banana Patch' Rastafarian rag dolls, pretty embroidery, and tasty Jamaican cookies. The colourful **market** is on one side of Mandeville Square, and operates from Monday to Saturday.

Sports

Mandeville boasts the Caribbean's oldest golf club: the **Manchester Club** has a nine-green (18-tee) golf course as well as tennis and billiards. **Manchester Golf Week** is in July.

This countryside is perfect for horse-riding, and it can be

arranged through Countrystyle at the Astra Country Inn. The **Jamaica Horse Association's Mandeville Show** is in July. Ask your hotel for details of other sports facilities.

◆◆◆
TREASURE BEACH

This lost and lazy corner of the coast has an away-from-it-all charm which is hard to beat. Life here is centred around the beaches. The main one is Frenchman's Bay, a curving stretch of biscuit-coloured sand, fringed by a few palms. Set in gardens on the dunes behind is a hotel and a variety of villas with rooms to rent. Colourful fishing canoes are drawn up on the beach, with names like Love Bird and Dandy Girl. Fishermen tend their boats and fishing cages; while a few Rastas, hippies and visitors sit chatting in one of the palm-thatched bars. The undertow on this beach can be tricky – neighbouring Calabash Bay is safer for bathing. Between the

cliffs and rocky points along this coast, there are other unspoilt sandy coves. Some have flat reefs lying just offshore which makes swimming difficult, but reef-walking is a popular pastime to look at the marine life. The rhythm of life at Treasure Beach is seriously relaxed. It's a wonderful place just to wander along the sands beside the turquoise sea, picking up pretty shells, or loll in a hammock watching the fiery sun sink below the horizon, bathing all in a magical glow. The settlement is scattered along the narrow road behind the beaches, where goats roam everywhere nibbling the bushes. Splashes of colour in this dry scrub and savannah landscape are provided by blossom on trees and vivid cascades of bougainvillea around many houses. A patchwork of cultivated vegetable plots can be seen on the coastal plain and slopes of the Santa Cruz Mountains rising just to the east.

The simple life is what Treasure Beach is all about – and that

The Manchester Golf Club

means few facilities. For anything other than basic necessities (including a bank), you will have to visit shops in a nearby town such as Black River. Horse-riding is available from the **Mayfield Ranch** at Southfield, about nine miles (14km) east, near the soaring cliffs of Lover's Leap. There is also a lively local disco, **Abba Garden**, 14 miles (22km) east at Junction. For further information, tours and accommodation advice, contact **Everything Nice Vacations and Tours** at Treasure Beach (tel: 965 0482), or the Tourist Board office in Black River. Many visitors just turn up at Treasure Beach and find a room on the spot.

Accommodation

The **Treasure Beach Hotel** (tel: 965 0110) has sparkling white buildings set amid flowery gardens on a hillock behind the beach; steps lead down to terraces around the pool. The attractive public rooms are open to the views and breezes; the bedrooms are quite simple, and in separate blocks – rates are moderate. There is a good variety of guest houses, villas and rooms in the area, at budget prices. Sitting on a rocky headland east of Calabash Bay, **Olde Wharf Resort** (tel: 962 4471 to book) is classed as a guest house but is like a hotel in size and facilities; modern and comfortable, it has a pool and fine views from the roof terrace. **Four Ms Cottage** (tel: 965 0131) is a neat, very homely guest house run by the inestimable Effie Campbell – you can eat in her kitchen. The **Siwind Guest House** (no phone) has a well-designed, spacious sitting room and kitchen, with simple bedrooms; it is set in leafy grounds on high land above the sea, with wonderful views and a private cove below. Lying in pretty gardens overlooking Calabash Bay are the pleasant, well-furnished **Sunset Resort Villas** (tel: 965 0143). **Nuestra Casa** (tel: 965 0152) is a comfortable house with character – like the charming northern English landlady who lets one of her rooms.

A haven of tranquillity at Treasure Beach

At Fort Charles, beside the sea a few miles northwest, is the **Unforgettable Inn** (tel: 990 6077, or in the US 203-621 4908), stylishly simple, it offers beautiful views, deserted beaches, complete peace and seclusion; facilities include a pool and tours by arrangement.

Restaurants

The **Yabba** restaurant at the Treasure Beach Hotel and the **Olde Wharf** restaurant (tel: 965 0003) are both good. The **Sea Crab** (tel: 963 0400), at the nearby fishing village of Great Bay, is a simple bar and restaurant serving delicious specialities like lobster at reasonable prices.

WHAT ELSE TO SEE IN THE SOUTHWEST

◆
ALLIGATOR POND

This sleepy fishing village is set on the coast 22 miles (35km) south of Mandeville, with mountains lying behind. To the west is **Wards Bay Country Village**, a recreation area with log cabins, picnic spots, and natural attractions such as Arawak caves. Alligator Pond has a beige-sand beach, where local boys surf on planks of wood. A rough track follows the coast east, and around Long Bay the deserted beach is backed by slopes of cacti-strewn rocks and scrub. **Gut River** is a pretty place, totally unspoilt and peaceful with a few fishing canoes drawn up on the beach. Nearby is God's Well, a 160-foot (49m) deep sinkhole with clear turquoise water.

THE APPLETON ESTATE RUM DISTILLERY

This is the oldest and biggest distillery in Jamaica, dating back around 250 years. The estate lies deep in the interior, about 27 miles (43km) northwest of Mandeville, splendidly set in a flat green valley beside Black River, which is covered in an extensive sea of sugar cane fields. The reception area is built in plantation-house style, and has a bar and souvenir shop for you to taste and buy the goodies. There are piles of burnt sugar cane beside the factory yard (the fields are burnt before harvesting, to make cutting the cane easier); and a smell of molasses pervades the air. There is a short tour of the distillery, which begins by showing visitors an old press drawn by a donkey. You are shown the huge stills, and the aging room full of oak barrels – the quality of the rum depends on how long it has been matured. A popular way to visit the Appleton Distillery is on the Appleton Express from Montego Bay which includes a buffet lunch.
Open: Monday to Saturday 09.00–17.00hrs.

APPLE VALLEY PARK

This picturesque leisure park is at Maggotty, a village on the banks of the Black River, about three miles (5km) west of Appleton. The village is much prettier than its name suggests and winds around a deep bend in the river, below a verdant wooded hill. The park covers

465 acres (188 hectares) of unspoilt countryside, and visitors may walk through the tropical forest full of colourful birds to see the Black River Gorge with its cascading waterfalls, or picnic in a grove of coconut palms. Attractions include a canoe ride down river, pedalo rides on one of the ponds, fishing for red snapper, silver perch and carp (which can be cooked and eaten here) or a tour up to the Maroon village of Accompong in Cockpit Country. The park also offers a variety of entertainments such as concerts or shows, and films on Sunday evenings. There is a restaurant serving Jamaican dishes, and accommodation in a guest house by the river, in a hilltop Great House, or camping (tents are available). For information contact Lucille and Patrick Lee, Sweet Bakery, PO Box 22, Maggotty, St Elizabeth.

◆
BAMBOO AVENUE

For a few miles along the main road, huge hundred-year-old bamboo plants gracefully arch their feathery fronds in a canopy over the road, to form a shady, sun-dappled green tunnel. Just to the east is a straggling village, which is a centre for growing cashew nuts: **West Lacovia**, **East Lacovia** and **Lacovia Tombstone**. Beside the road here are the graves of two English soldiers, who died fighting a duel over a woman in 1723. One of them was an ancestor of Princess Diana, and you can see the Spencer-Althorp coat of arms on the

gravestone. To the west of Bamboo Avenue is **Middle Quarters**, where women sell delicious hot peppered shrimp by the roadside. It lies about 30 miles (48km) west of Mandeville.

◆◆◆
BLACK RIVER SAFARI ✓

The Black River is Jamaica's longest, and a peaceful half-hour boat trip takes you along the river through part of the island's most extensive wetland. The guide, Charles Swaby, is an expert on the history, flora, fauna and delicate ecological balance of the area, which makes it a fascinating trip. There are dense mangrove thickets along the banks, putting down tangles of roots into the river; pancake water lilies and floating water hyacinths – which bloom bluey-mauve in spring – carpet the water.

You may sometimes see fires smoking in the surrounding wetlands as the peaty soil gives off methane gas, which ignites spontaneously; the vegetation grows so quickly it soon looks green again. The peat soil makes the river water look black, although it is actually crystal clear.

The birdlife along the river is a delight. Ospreys (sea eagles) can sometimes be seen hovering overhead ready to pounce on a fish. There are also several varieties of heron, and delicate jacana birds walking on the waterlilies.

When it starts getting hot, crocodiles bask in their favourite spots along the water's

edge. Apart from many varities of fish, the river has long been an important source of crayfish. Fishermen still use traditional methods of catching them with conical funnel-shaped traps woven of split bamboo – this design originally came from Africa. They are baited and laid in the water, and the spot is marked with the fisherman's individual sign, such as a particular knot tied in a bullrush.

The boat leaves from by the road bridge on the east side of Black River, 43 miles (69km) southwest of Mandeville. South Coast Safaris can also arrange other trips, including coastal wetland tours, photographic safaris, bird watching and wildlife tours, fishing trips and canoe or rowing boat rentals. The Black River Safari boat tour runs four times a day; if you are most interested in the birdlife go at 09.00 or 16.00hrs; to see crocodiles go at 11.00 or 14.00hrs.

Taking a trip on Black River

◆◆
BLUEFIELDS TO SCOTT'S COVE

This tranquil stretch of coast lying eight to 20 miles (13 to 32km) northwest of Black River, has several pretty, unspoilt beaches. Before Scott's Cove a dirt track leads off the main road to **Fonthill Beach**, a tiny cove of silvery sand with clear aquamarine waters bathing the reef. **Scott's Cove** is a delightful rocky cove and creek, where a river runs into the sea. Fishermen moor their traditional dugout canoes here, and can be seen mending them or making their fishing cages. Meanwhile, women fry the freshly caught fish on open fires – which they sell with bammy at roadside stalls. The wafting aromas are mouthwatering.

A little further, just past Whitehouse, is the **Cotton Tree Beach Park**. A tiny stretch of silver sand is backed by a garden with picnic tables and a bar serving snacks. There are swings for children and watersports are available. The beach is shallow, and the reef lies close to the shore, so although it is a good place for children to paddle, it is not easy for swimming – which would be better from the neighbouring rocky coves.

The scenery becomes more green, wooded and hilly along the coast road here – especially approaching **Bluefields**, which is a very picturesque area. The limpid turquoise sea of Bluefields Bay bathes its curve of white sands; it was from here that Henry Morgan and his fleet sailed to sack Panama in 1670. There are splendid drives up into the mountains inland, with destinations such as the sleepy market and tobacco-growing town of Darliston.

◆
LOVER'S LEAP

Where the Santa Cruz Mountains meet the coast, this escarpment plunges 1,500 feet (457m) directly down to the greeny-blue sea below. There is a lighthouse at the top, and the views along the coast are really wonderful – but looking down the sheer cliffs can be quite dizzying.

◆◆◆
MARSHALL'S PEN ✓

This splendid 18th-century Great House used to be a huge coffee estate. Now it is a 300-acre (121-hectare) cattle farm set amid rolling green hills, with fields surrounded by drystone walls and woods. You are shown around this private home like a welcome guest, and regaled with many stories and facts about Jamaica. The house is mostly built of wood, and has many beautiful antiques, *objets d'art*, and interesting artefacts to admire. These include a fine 17th-century chair, decorative pieces from India, Arawak stone tools, and an exquisite collection of shells. The walls are adorned with portraits of distinguished ancestors, family photographs and pretty botanical paintings. It is surrounded by charming gardens, where you can see the terraces on which coffee beans were dried (called barbecues). It is a magnificent area for walking and bird watching – the grounds are a bird sanctuary. The house is on the northwest outskirts of Mandeville, and tours can be arranged through local hotels such as the Astra, or by contacting Marshall's Pen, PO Box 58, Mandeville.

A dizzy plunge: Lover's Leap

Lover's Leap Lighthouse

where he bathed his wounds in a salty spring; seeing the miraculous cure, his owner promised no more punishment if he showed him where it was. On his death, the owner willed the property to the government for the benefit of the people. The mineral spring water is reputed to be the most radioactive in the world, and recommended for rheumatism, eczema, and numerous other complaints. There is a modest hotel with spa facilities, including an outdoor mineral swimming pool.
Open: daily 07.00–21.00hrs.
Just west of here is Canoe Valley, known for its colony of manatees (sea cows), a rare marine mammal. At **Alligator Hole River** you can take a canoe ride to see these affable creatures.

◆
SAVANNA-LA-MAR
The name of this undistinguished market town and port means 'plain by the sea'. Its bustling wharf lies at the end of Great George Street, near the remaining walls of an old fort which now form an improvised swimming pool. Along this street you can see the 19th-century courthouse with its ornate drinking fountain and a variety of pavement stalls.
Near the sugar centre of Frome, six miles (10km) north, the Roaring River emerges through rocks from underground; this is a popular and scenic spot for bathing and picnicking.
Savanna-la-Mar lies about 20 miles (32km) from Negril.

◆
MILK RIVER BATH
This mineral spa lies in a quiet rural setting beside the Milk River, about 30 miles (48km) southeast of Mandeville. The therapeutic value of these waters was apparently discovered by a badly beaten slave who ran off to the hills,

◆◆◆
YS FALLS ✓

Set in a beautiful green valley surrounded by rolling wooded hills, YS Falls are idyllically unspoilt – as nature intended – and could well be the most entrancing of Jamaica's waterfalls. About 33 miles (53km) west of Mandeville, turn off the main road at Holland, and after driving a short way up a rough lane, there is a bar selling tickets. Visitors are taken to the falls by tractor-drawn wagon (or on foot), across meadows scattered with trees. The only sounds to be heard are the birdsong and the splash of water cascading over the golden rocks. You can bathe in the crystal-clear greenish pools, picnic, swim or simply sit and soak up the scenery. The falls are best visited in the morning, as clouds tend to gather as the day goes on.

Open: daily 08.00–20.00hrs.

Natural grace at YS Falls

PEACE AND QUIET

A fiery Jamaican sunset

Countryside and Wildlife in Jamaica
by Paul Sterry

For those simply seeking relaxation and peace and quiet, Jamaica makes an ideal destination. However, for those who also have an interest in natural history, the island is a paradise. More than 250 species of bird have been recorded, of which 25 species and 21 sub-species are endemic; in other words they are found nowhere else in the world. In common with Jamaica's butterflies and flowers, many of the birds are extremely colourful, as one might imagine in so idyllic a place.

White sand beaches backed by groves of palm trees make the island a living picture of the ideal tropical island. In places around the coast there are also marshes and swamps, while, inland, there are steep mountains covered in luxuriant forest. Much of the original forest in the lowland areas has long since gone, cleared and replaced by the cultivation of crops such as mangos, bananas and sugar cane.

The Coast

For most holiday visitors, the glorious, sandy beaches are Jamaica's crowning glory. However, the island's coastline is far from uniform; there are coastal lagoons, mudflats and mangroves, especially along the south coast, and rocky shores with offshore coral reefs along the northern coast. Each habitat attracts different types of wildlife, so there is always something to see wherever you are along the coast.

From the point of view of anyone interested in natural history, sandy beaches have least to offer, since they have few food resources and no shelter. However, above the

PEACE AND QUIET

Brown pelican

tide-line, washed-up seashells can provide hours of interest since there are so many different species to look for. Also, land crabs can be found on the coconut palms. Mudflats are rich in invertebrates, so when exposed at low tide, they provide better feeding for birds and consequently better opportunities for the birdwatcher; look for egrets, herons, waders and terns. Further offshore, coral reefs are also extremely productive and many cays are located off Kingston, Negril and Portland on the south coast.

Mangroves are an important habitat for many forms of wildlife. The salt-tolerant trees that make up the swamps tolerate immersion in seawater and exposure to air on a twice-daily basis with the tides. Their complex root-systems trap mud and help to consolidate new land. Fiddler crabs and other crustaceans are abundant and form the basis of the food web here. Mangroves are important

Brown Pelican

Brown pelicans are common around the coasts, often displaying little fear of humans. They may look rather cumbersome on the ground, but in the air they are skilled and elegant flyers. This is the only species of pelican that dives to catch its food. If a shoal of fish is located, up to a dozen birds may gather in the vicinity, plunge-diving into the water, their throat pouches inflating to engulf the prey. Juvenile brown pelicans have mottled brown plumage. Adults, however, are more striking and have attractive markings on the head and neck. During the breeding season, the cap and lower neck are creamy buff while the nape of the neck is chestnut. Pelicans nest in mangroves from December until June.

nurseries for the young stages of many oceanic fish species.

The Blue Mountains

The Blue Mountains dominate eastern Jamaica. Much of the area is still cloaked in forest that is home to many of Jamaica's birds, although forestry and coffee plantations are regrettably depleting the natural vegetation. The main peaks lie along the Grand Ridge and include Blue Mountain Peak, at 7,402 feet (2,255m) the highest mountain in Jamaica.

The easiest point of access is from the Kingston–Newcastle–Buff Bay road; between Newcastle and Hardwar Gap, the forest is excellent. There are numerous trails leading from Newcastle itself and to the north of the town in the Hollywell Park.

Continuing along the road to Buff Bay from Newcastle, turn off towards Westphalia and nearby are the Cinchona Botanical Gardens; to reach these English-style gardens, which are in the heart of a coffee-growing area, requires a steep hike from the road. Reaching the summit of Blue Mountain Peak requires considerable effort and a degree of planning; information can be obtained from the Jamaica Tourist Board.

Luxuriant forests of blue mahoe – the national tree of Jamaica – and mahogany cover the mountains. Tree ferns and epiphytic orchids and bromeliads thrive in the humidity and colourful butterflies abound.

Hummingbirds

Jamaica has four species of hummingbirds, all of which are reasonably common and widespread. These delightful little birds are the only group that hover habitually, their wings looking like a blur of colour. Although they occasionally take insects, they feed for the most part on nectar, collecting it from flowers while on the wing; in the process they transfer pollen from one flower to another and are important agents of pollination for many of Jamaica's flowers. At only 2½ inches (6cm) in length, the vervain hummingbird is the smallest species on the island. The plumage is mainly green and the female has a white-tipped tail. There are two species of streamertail – black-billed and red-billed – males of which have long tail streamers. Lastly, the Jamaican mango is comparatively large at 5 inches (13cm) in length. The plumage is mainly dark, although a reddish sheen can be seen on the head in certain lights. Hummingbirds build delicate little nests from lichens and cobwebs. Although in themselves the eggs are small, in relation to the size of the bird that produced them they are among the largest in the bird kingdom.

Hellshire Hills

This region of arid limestone terrain cloaked in dense cactus scrub lies south of Spanish Town, within easy reach of Kingston. Popular sandy beaches can be found on the road to Fort Clarence and

Hellshire Point, but the interior of the hills is largely inaccessible because of the impenetrable scrub. Salt lagoons and mangrove swamps can be found along the road to Hellshire Point - look for herons, ibises and waders.

Marshall's Pen

Marshall's Pen is a private cattle ranch and nature reserve on the northwest outskirts of Mandeville (see page 100). Twenty-three of Jamaica's endemic birds have been seen in the limestone forest that surrounds the farm.

Cockpit Country

South of Falmouth, this is an area of extraordinary limestone scenery, known as *karst,* where, over millions of years, gentle erosion by mildly acidic rainwater has carved bizarre conical shapes and sinkholes. Much of the terrain is covered in wet forest and is, to all intents and purposes, inaccessible to all but the most experienced and determined. However, rough roads wind around its fringes. Highlights to look out for include parrots, now rare because of the depredations of collectors.

Black River Morass

At the coastal town of Black River, in the southwest, the Broad River and the Black River have created the Great Morass, the most extensive wetland on the island. The Upper Morass has been partly drained and altered, while the Lower Morass, nearest to the town, remains largely unaffected.

The coastline of the Lower Morass is fringed with mangroves which gradually give way inland, under increasingly freshwater conditions, to saltgrass marsh and finally wetland forest. This is the haunt of herons, ibises, West Indian whistling ducks and waders.

American crocodiles, although scarce, are regularly seen on boat trips into the swamps from Black River, and manatees – rare and docile marine mammals that graze sea grasses – are sometimes seen at the mouth of the rivers. Despite drainage, many wetland birds can still be seen on Upper Morass, and the area can be viewed from the roads which surround it between Elim, Newton, East Lacovia and Wilton. Visitors should also drive southeast from Black River on the road to Pondside and on to Treasure Beach. There are ponds beside the road between Pondside

---

Migrant Waders

Known to North American birdwatchers as shorebirds, waders such as sandpipers and plovers are common around the coast and on the wetlands at certain times of year. Although a few species are resident, many more are visitors arriving in September and staying until March. These migrant waders breed mostly in North America's arctic region but could not survive winters there. Jamaica's warm climate and abundance of marine and freshwater life suits them ideally.

heads bordered with a white half-collar, dark upperparts and pale underparts. White-chinned thrushes on the other hand, have mainly dark plumage with a white spot on the wings and under the 'chin' and an attractive orange bill and legs.

Ocho Rios

Despite its popularity, there are plenty of opportunities to observe wildlife around Ocho Rios. The Shaw Park Gardens can be reached by heading south on the A3 and after a short distance turning right at the Anglican Church. Here visitors will find waterfalls, beautiful gardens, hummingbirds and many other birds. By heading south on the A3, the visitor soon drives

Bananaquits on a coffee plant

and Williamsfield, Great Pedro Pond near Treasure Beach is good for ducks, grebes and waders.

Rocklands Bird Sanctuary and Feeding Station

Birdwatchers will certainly want to visit the Rocklands Bird Sanctuary (see page 36), which is just east of Anchovy, south of Montego Bay. Birds come here to be fed and many are incredibly tame. Three species of hummingbird can be seen: red-billed streamertails, vervain hummingbirds and Jamaican mangos. Visitors should also look for white-eyed thrushes and white-chinned thrushes. The former have prominent white eyes, brown

American Crocodile
American crocodiles are widespread in the warm seas of the Caribbean although they have become rather scarce because of persecution. They can grow to an immense size – often over 12 feet (4m) in length – and prefer to live in coastal waters and estuaries. Crocodiles spend much of their time in water with only the nose and eyes exposed to the air, although they do occasionally sunbathe. Females lay a clutch of eggs in soft sand beside the water and these are incubated by the warmth of the sun. American crocodiles can be distinguished from alligators because the fourth tooth on the lower jaw can still be seen when the mouth is closed.

PEACE AND QUIET

through Fern Gully, one of the best places on the island to see a variety of species of these attractive plants. To the west of Ocho Rios is the Dunn's River Falls, the best known and most spectacular waterfall on the island.

Eastern Jamaica

The eastern coast is one of the most dramatic and scenic parts of the island, and the coast road, from Port Antonio to Morant Bay, allows easy exploration of the area. Heading southeast from Port Antonio, visitors reach the Blue Hole, an impressive but very popular tourist spot. As you continue around the coast, look for seabirds offshore, including white-tailed tropic birds between Machioneal and Hector's River. These graceful birds have white plumage and boast extremely long tail streamers. Sea birds can also be seen from near Morant Point Lighthouse, Jamaica's most southeasterly point.

Frigatebirds
Magnificent frigatebirds are a familiar sight in the skies around the coast of Jamaica. These masters of the air have a wingspan over seven feet (2m) and effortlessly ride the sea breezes, using their long, forked tails to help control their direction. Sometimes called 'Man O' War' birds, frigatebirds are aerial pirates: although they sometimes scavenge dead fish and occasionally pick live ones from the surface of the water, most of their diet is obtained by harassing pelicans and other sea birds into disgorging their last meal. For their size, frigatebirds are lightweight; this helps minimise the effort required to remain airborne. Male frigatebirds have all-black plumage with a bright red throat sac. When displaying to attract a female, this is inflated and is an extraordinary sight, especially when several males are nesting in the same area.

Shaw Park Gardens

FOOD AND DRINK

Visitors attracted by the beaches and the climate may not have realised that Jamaican cuisine can make eating one of the greatest pleasures of their holiday. Like so many aspects of life on the island, it derives much from the rich blend of cultural influences – from African to Arawak Indian, Spanish to Chinese, East Indian to English – as well as having a uniquely piquant Jamaican flavour. The island it blessed with a wide variety of fruit and vegetables, and its waters yield a wealth of fish and seafood. You can eat well in the smallest roadside restaurant – bars and snack shacks – where standards of cleanliness and hygiene are high, so do not be put of even if they look shabby. You can often eat better (and much more cheaply) at many of the simple Jamaican guest houses than in sophisticated hotels – both of which serve meals to non-residents, except the all-inclusive hotels.

In a small local restaurant there is usually a blackboard with the day's menu displayed – which depends on what they managed to buy in the market or from the fishermen that morning. Food is often cooked to order and served at Jamaican pace, but usually worth the wait. As everywhere, there are also fast-food places to suit American and European impatience. Beside the road, you will notice the rondavel bars (a round or polygonal building with a pointed roof and sides that are open to breezes), which serve good snacks like jerk pork or chicken. In this climate, many restaurants have open-air terraces and patios. There is a variety of specialist restaurants too, such as Chinese or Rastafarian (*ital* vegetarian food). Ackee and salt fish is Jamaica's national dish – typically served for breakfast, but also as a snack at any time. Ackee is a bright red fruit that is seen growing on trees all over the island – first brought here by Captain Bligh. It has to be allowed to ripen and open up naturally – to reveal three large black seeds set in lobes of yellow flesh, which is then boiled, otherwise it is poisonous. Cooked with salted cod (originally imported as a cheap source of protein for the slaves), and often mixed with onions and peppers, it's delicious – remarkably like scrambled eggs.

For breakfast and other meals you may also see 'run down' (run dun), which is mackerel, shad or salted cod simmered in boiled-down coconut milk, often with onions and peppers. Liver is another sustaining dish served for Jamaica-style breakfast. Fried slices of plantain are often served on the side at breakfast or other meals. Hotels offer traditional, European or American dishes at breakfast, but the menu may also include fresh tropical fruit, and sweet things like cinnamon cakes or banana bread. Guava jelly and logwood honey are Jamaican alternatives to marmalade. Brown bread (and brown sugar) are almost never seen in Jamaica, though they have a type of bread called

FOOD AND DRINK

hard-dough (hardo) with a very close, hard texture.

Soup is very popular in local restaurants and is often automatically served before the main course, without being ordered, Staple spicy soups include pumpkin, pepperpot and red pea (bean) soup. Manish water is a highly-seasoned thick soup based on green bananas and goat offal. Fish soup is frequently called fish tea. The seafood is superb. There is a wonderful variety of fresh fish, such as kingfish (usually served in steaks), various snapper (including red and yellow fin) and jack (rather like fresh pilchard). They are cooked in a variety of ways; some small restaurants, including shacks by the roadside or beaches, cook traditionally on open-fire stoves (such as at Hellshire Beach and Scott's Cove in the south). Fried fish is generally not at all greasy, more like grilled fish, and is often eaten with bammy – fried cassava bread. Escovitched fish is sautéed in a spicy sauce (a method derived from the Spanish). Peppered shrimp are

Bright bites at a jerk pork bar

a delicious delicacy of the Black River area.

Curried dishes, especially goat curry, are popular, and full of flavour (a way of cooking that Indian workers introduced). More conservative meat-eaters will easily find beef on menus. Roast suckling pig is another local speciality well worth trying, as is the jerk pork. Hot and spicy, it is traditionally cooked over a fire of pimento wood, which lies in a hollow or 'pit' – the most authentic and best is said to come from around Boston Bay, although it is sold everywhere. This method of cooking is thought to have originated from the Arawak Indians, and passed on to the Maroons. 'Jerk' comes from a Spanish word meaning to prepare the pork like the Quechua Indians of South America. You will also see jerk chicken, and fish. Jerk pork and other snacks are often eaten with fried dumplings, called festival or johnny cakes.

In local restaurants main courses are typically served

with rice 'n' peas (white rice with red kidney beans, or occasionally green gunga peas, cooked in coconut milk) – such a staple food that it has been dubbed 'the Jamaican coat-of-arms'. Sweet potato is particularly good with curries; green banana, breadfruit and yam are bland, starchy vegetables which are fine with spicy foods. Green vegetables include callaloo (spinach), okra (ladies' fingers) and chocho (pear-shaped with a pale green, prickly skin and a taste like marrow).

For dessert, try the romantically-named matrimony: a delectable blend of orange and star apple pulp mixed with cream, sugar and nutmeg. Guava cheese is a sweet chewy jelly.

The wealth of fruit available is a mouthwatering delight: pineapple, pawpaw (papaya), bananas, mango, guava, watermelon, passion fruit and many others not found in supermarkets at home – succulent fruits sounding and tasting exotic. Star apples are a sweet, round purple fruit, with seeds set in a star pattern when cut. Ortaniques are a cross between an orange and a tangerine – Jamaica has successfully produced many hybrid citrus fruits.

Snacks which may be unfamiliar include Solomon Grundy, a spiced pickled herring often served as an appetizer, as is tasty smoked marlin. Stamp-and-go are crispy batter-fried salt codfish fritters; the name comes from an old nautical command that used to be given to sailors. Cakes and pastries are popular, such as plantain tarts or coconut gizzardas. If you visit a Jamaican home you may be offered a slice of rich, fruity Christmas cake – so heavily laced with rum it improves with age. Locals often chew on a length of sugar cane – usually larger and softer than the cane used to make sugar and rum – bought from wayside stalls.

Drinks

Starting with the strong stuff: Jamaica equals rum. There is a wide range of different colours, tastes and strengths – Appleton is the most famous brand. Gold rum has a light, smooth flavour

A hearty Jamaican breakfast

FOOD AND DRINK

which is good for drinking on the rocks. The longer the rum has been matured in oak barrels, the mellower (and more expensive) it becomes. Many Jamaicans drink the potent white overproof rum – tradition has it that the first gulp opens the eyes, the second closes them. Rum is also used in many delicious cocktails, like Planter's Punch. These are frequently very sweet, so if you prefer them less so ask the barman to hold back (or leave out) the syrup. Jamaican liqueurs include coffee-flavoured Tia Maria, a rum liqueur called Rumona, and Sangster's Old Jamaica liqueurs which are blended with rum and come in several varieties such as Blue Mountain coffee, ginger and ortanique. The most popular local beer is Red Stripe. Imported wines tend to be expensive, but there are wines made in Jamaica from imported pulp – Monterey and the slightly drier Rhine Valley are white wines reminiscent of popular German wines.

With such a profusion of fresh fruit, there is also an exciting choice of non-alcoholic fruit cocktails. A traditional soft drink is sorrel, made from the bright red parts of a flower, which is flavoured with ginger – it tastes like ginger-blackcurrant squash. Soursop is also an old favourite, made from a rough-skinned fruit of that name, and reputed to be an aphrodisiac. Irish Moss is a healthy blend of processed seaweed (agar), condensed milk, vanilla and nutmeg – an alleged aid to sexual prowess. A typical local thirst-quencher is coconut water, drunk straight from the green coconut. Water is generally served with meals, and is quite safe to drink from the tap. Remember that in a hot

Crafts with character – the Royal Dwarf Factory

climate it is advisable to drink plenty of liquid – without alcohol.

Jamaica's Blue Mountain coffee is renowned for its strong, aromatic flavour; make sure you ask for it, as many places simply serve instant.

SHOPPING

Jamaican handicrafts are widely sold in the north coast resorts – and at stalls along the roadside. All the main resorts and towns visited by tourists have their craft market, selling goods such as wooden carvings, woven straw hats and baskets, tie-dyed clothes, shell jewellery, or beads and belts in Rasta colours. Do not buy jewellery made from black coral or from turtles since both of these are protected. In these markets you should haggle to buy at a good price, but do not be hassled into buying souvenirs you don't want; the 'higglers' are expert at high-pressure selling both in these markets and on the street. If you are self-catering, it is well worth visiting the ordinary fruit and vegetable markets. But even if you are not buying, these bustling street markets make for a colourful taste of real Jamaica – and there is less hassle, as the food markets cater for locals rather than tourists.

Traditionally, market traders are usually women – called 'higglers' since colonial times, though today this also refers to any street hawkers. Details on craft markets are given under individual resorts, along with shops where you can find some higher quality Jamaican art. Two picturesque places to find some attractive gifts, including arts and crafts, are Devon House in Kingston and Harmony Hall near Ocho Rios.

The vogue in Jamaica, as in so many places, is for modern shopping plazas. Some of these are aimed specifically at tourists, with shops selling duty-free goods and up-market boutiques; other centres have more everyday shops. Banks, pharmacies and supermarkets can often be found in or around one of the shopping plazas. The duty-free shops are widely advertised.

(Shopping information is given under individual resorts; for shop opening hours, see page 123 in the **Directory**.)

Popular souvenirs worth taking home from Jamaica include rum (naturally), local liqueurs such as Tia Maria or Sangster's Old Jamaica, Blue Mountain coffee, reggae tapes or records, and local art and crafts such as wood carvings.

ACCOMMODATION

The main resorts have an excellent range of accommodation. In the south the choice is much more limited. Generally the standard of accommodation is high, and prices at many of the main resort hotels reflect this. However, the variety of inexpensive accommodation is not widely publicised; tour operators often use certain standard hotels, and tend to exclude the cheaper ones. If you are looking for low-priced hotels or guest houses, you will

ACCOMMODATION

Greengrocer, Montego Bay

probably have to book independently. You can make your stay in Jamaica reasonably inexpensive if you are prepared to be flexible and a bit adventurous. Most hotel prices are lower in summer – except in Kingston. Check whether quoted hotel rates include the General Consumption Tax of 15 per cent; a 10 per cent service charge is usually added to the bill as well. Rates for all-inclusive hotels normally have the extra charges already included.

The popular tourist hotels tend to have an American approach (for instance, half-board is called MAP, modified American plan), and prices are quoted in US dollars. There has been a boom in all-inclusive hotels, where everything – from sports to tips, and even drinks in most places – is 'free' after paying the initial all-in price. This may sound like a good deal, but it discourages guests from setting foot outside the hotel. If all you are interested in is the beach, with hot and cold running sports and activities all day long, then this may be ideal. Many of the larger hotels are attractively designed, and set around lovely tropical gardens, often with a private beach. Even the simplest accommodation is usually very clean, and service is typically willing and friendly.

Some hotel groups allow visitors staying at one hotel to use others in the same group. For instance, Sandals' guests can use the facilities at all their hotels (in Montego Bay, Ocho Rios and Negril). Elegant Resorts International offer arrangements for their guests to eat or stay at any of their properties (Half Moon, Round Hill and Coyaba near Montego Bay, Good Hope south of Falmouth, Plantation Inn at Ocho Rios and Trident by Port Antonio).

Jamaica also has a wide range of self-catering accommodation, from modest rooms with a kitchenette or hot-plate and fridge, to sumptuous villas with a maid to cook and clean.

The Tourist Board has a list of 'approved' hotels and guest houses. But places not included are not necessarily below Tourist Board standards; some do not bother to register, for example. Check with the Tourist Board about which of the larger hotels have a booking agent in this country. Information on both hotels and self-catering properties, and an independent booking service, is offered by The Caribbean Centre, 3 The Green, Richmond, Surrey TW9 1PL (tel: 0181-940 3399). Information on self-catering accommodation is also available from the Tourist Board, or the Jamaica Association of Villas and Apartments (JAVA) at Pineapple Place, PO Box 298, Ocho Rios (tel: 974 2508).

An alternative to traditional resort accommodation is provided by Countrystyle, which arranges personalised holidays in rural guest houses, private homes or villas, where you can get to know the culture and people of Jamaica. It covers the island, but specialises in southern and central areas. Countrystyle is based at the Astra Country Inn, PO Box 60, Mandeville (tel: 962 3265). For information on budget lodgings, cabins and campsites contact the Tourist Board, or Peter Bentley, Maya Lodge, PO Box 216, Kingston 7 (tel: 927 2097).

NIGHTLIFE AND ENTERTAINMENT

Much of the island's nightlife is based around the main tourist resorts and hotels – and in these spots, you'll be able to give your dancing shoes a good workout. Larger hotels, especially the all-inclusives, have nightly entertainment – anything from a calypso singer to a live band, fashion show or the full works with limbo-dancing and fire-eating. Some of the discos, nightclubs and other evening entertainments are listed under individual resorts. Being the cultural centre of Jamaica, Kingston has a wide choice of entertainment. Outside the main resorts and towns, there may not be much to do at night apart from hang out at the local bar – which can turn out to be quite an entertainment in itself.

WEATHER AND WHEN TO GO

Winter and summer seasons are a bit of a misnomer in Jamaica as temperatures throughout the year only vary within a range of around 80°F (27°C) to 90°F

Poolside drinks at the Wyndham Rose Hall hotel (see page 23)

(32°C). The coolest months are December to March; the driest February and March. It is wettest in early summer (May to June) and autumn (September to October), but only to the extent of daily tropical showers – usually short, heavy and warm. There is quite a variance in local climate on the island due to the central backbone of mountains, which divides the relatively humid and rainy north coast from the drier southern districts. The highest annual rainfall is found in the northeast of the island. Humidity is generally high, but mercifully tempered by a cool tradewind off the ocean, known as the Doctor Breeze, during the day, and an evening wind from the mountains, the ominously named Undertaker's Breeze. If the heat and humidity gets too much, a trip to the interior highlands should bring relief with temperatures 10°F (5·5°C) to 20°F (11°C) lower than those on the coast. A local rhyme has

this to say about hurricanes: 'June, too soon. July, stand by. August, prepare you must. September, remember. October, all over'. Hurricanes in June, July or October tend to last for around a week; in August and September they can run for a fortnight. If the situation is serious, the Office of Disaster Preparedness and Emergency Relief Coordination (ODIPERC) will broadcast warnings and instructions on television and radio. High season in Jamaica is mid-December to April, particularly around Christmas and the New Year when hotel rooms, rental cars and beach space are at a premium.

HOW TO BE A LOCAL

Jamaicans are generally good natured and exuberant – they like to laugh a lot. You can have great fun returning their friendliness and chatting to them – they love to talk, too. However, in tourist resorts persistent hassling can be annoying; tourists equals money, and you have to remember that this is a poor country, and everyone is anxious to earn a crust. If you are being hassled to buy goods or services you don't want, just keep saying a polite but firm 'no, thank you'. Jamaicans appreciate directness; they are very direct themselves so do not find the blunt truth offensive. Misunderstandings are more likely to arise if you couch what you mean in evasiveness and equivocation. This does not mean you can be downright rude: as everywhere, good manners and a smile go a long

KINGSTON

May, June, August–October

December–March, July & August

way in oiling the wheels of social encounters. 'Do as you would be done by' is a motto tourists will find it advisable to adopt. In rural areas, Jamaicans are usually simply curious about white visitors. Contact with the locals on an equal basis can be a most rewarding experience. If you'd like an introduction, ask the Tourist Board about their (free) Meet The People scheme; and Diana McIntyre-Pike of the Astra Country Inn in Mandeville is also eager to put visitors in touch with locals.

Although some of the larger resorts and towns seem to be full of bustling activity, Jamaicans have an unruffled, relaxed attitude. 'No problem – this is Jamaica', they'll say. It overcomes the breakdowns and delays that inevitably occur in services such as buses and telephones – which in Western eyes seem to stem from lack of organisation. Even if there does seem to be a problem, they'll shrug and tell you 'no problem'. Since impatient demands for service and loud protestations will yield few results, your visit will be much more relaxing if you settle into the Jamaican pace of life – content in the knowledge that eventually most things 'soon come'.

Jamaicans may be relaxed, but there is one aspect of behaviour where anything does *not* go – or rather nothing, because that's nude sunbathing. Going topless has become acceptable, and is frequently seen on tourist beaches, although local women do not do it. Sunbathing in the nude will cause offence, except on certain private beaches that are reserved for the purpose. Women travelling on their own are more than likely to be approached by men who can become a pest. The Jamaicans are as direct about sex as everything else; if that's what they are after, they will ask you almost straight away if you want to 'spend the night' with them. Don't be coy, your response must be just as direct in order to

prevent misunderstandings. If the answer is 'no', don't try to let them down gently, as that is more likely to lead to trouble than saying so straight out.

The chances are you will be offered *ganja* (marijuana) or even cocaine. Just remember that these drugs are illegal, and if you are caught with any in your possession it could result in a hefty fine, deportation or even jail.

CHILDREN

Jamaicans love children – in fact, Jamaican women advise having lots, with or without a husband. Children are a good point of contact when striking up conversations with locals.

However, some of the smarter hotels do not accept children as guests – including some of the all-inclusive hotels which are for couples only, like the Sandals group. On the other hand, there are also all-inclusive hotels which are specifically aimed at families – with special packages and activities – such as Boscobel Beach not far from Ocho Rios, the Trelawny Beach Hotel at Falmouth (east of Montego Bay), and the Franklyn D Resort at Runaway Bay. Generally, children are more welcome at the smaller, less expensive hotels and guest houses – and in some of these, children under a certain age (12, for example) can stay in their parents' room free. Children might find some of the typical local dishes in Jamaica a bit spicy, but you can easily find food they will like – including fried chicken, burgers and fruity puddings. Plenty of fun can be had outdoors with watersports, swimming and sandcastles. You must watch out for sunburn, which can ruin a holiday. The sun in Jamaica is strong, and cooling breezes deceptive. Make sure you have T-shirts, sunhats and sunblock cream to hand. And don't let your

children stay out too long, especially in the first few days – the same goes for you.

TIGHT BUDGET TIPS

- Hotel prices out of season (May to December) are likely to be as much as 40% cheaper.

- The south is generally cheaper than the north.

- The big resorts are the most expensive, so stay and shop in the smaller places.

- You can eat more cheaply in restaurants than hotels.

- Shop around for car rental.

- Bring your own toiletries, film etc – as they are likely to cost more in Jamaica.

- Rates of exchange are cheaper in banks than hotels or *bureaux de change*.

SPORT

There are plenty of sporting activities to be found in the main resorts and at larger hotels. Watersports of every description reign supreme at Negril, Montego Bay and Ocho Rios, with a good variety also at Runaway Bay, Port Antonio and Kingston. You can go sailing, water-skiing, windsurfing, scuba diving, snorkelling, jet-skiing, para-sailing, deep-sea fishing, you name it. Other popular sports include golf and horse-riding. Details are given under individual resorts.

Contents

DIRECTORY

Arriving

Entry formalities

British visitors require a valid
10-year passport and return
ticket, but no visa, for stays of
up to six months; EU residents
can stay for up to three months
without a visa; North American
citizens can remain for up to six
months, and can replace the
passport requirement with two
documents from the following
list: residency card or
naturalisation certificate,
driver's licence with
photograph, voter's registration

*Getting about in style: jet-skiing in
Montego Bay*

card or birth certificate.
Married women will require
their marriage certificate if
producing a birth certificate
from the above list.

Airports

Jamaica has two international
airports. Kingston's Norman
Manley International Airport
serves the island's capital and
the resorts of Mandeville and
Port Antonio, while Montego
Bay has its own Donald
Sangster International Airport,

which is also more convenient for visitors to Negril and Ocho Rios.

Transport from the Airport
Taxis are readily available and suggested tariffs to various destinations are displayed in the airport building. Fares should be agreed before you set forth. If possible, it is best to arrange airport transportation to your hotel with a travel agent in advance. Although fares from the airports into Kingston or Montego Bay are reasonable, it will be far more costly to reach the outlying resorts.

Babysitting
Most hotels which take children can provide this service.

Bike Rental
Car rental (see below) is an expensive business in Jamaica, and outside the main centres public transport is pretty dire. If you are not planning on a major sightseeing expedition, a motorbike or moped could be the answer for local journeys. Most hotels can arrange bike rental.

Camping
There are several campsites in the Blue Mountains, and also around the main resorts. For information on sites, maps, treks, cabins and other budget accommodation contact:
Jamaica Alternative and Camping-Hiking Association (JACHA), Maya Lodge, Box 216, Kingston 7 (tel: 927 2097).

Car Rental
Car rental is expensive in Jamaica, and during the winter season it is sometimes difficult to get a rental car at short notice. It is advisable to book ahead at any time, and plan your sightseeing itinerary carefully to get best value for money. A major credit card imprint will suffice for a deposit; without one you may have to lodge upwards of J$3,000 in cash. Foreign driving licences are valid for up to three months; and there is a minimum age limit of 24 years. Most major car rental companies are represented on the island, so you can book before you leave home. They, and local companies, are listed in Jamaica's Yellow Pages telephone directory, and most have offices in Kingston, Montego Bay and the main resorts. Some useful numbers are:
Anna (tel: 953 2010)
Avis (tel: 926 1560)
Bargain (tel: 926 8021)
Budget (tel: 938 2189)
Fiesta (tel: 926 0133)
Island Car Rentals (tel: 926 8012)
Sunshine (tel: 952 4218)
United (tel: 952 3077)

Chemists see Pharmacies

Crime
Petty theft is a way of life in Jamaica, and the locals suffer too. Thefts are rarely violent, but unguarded possessions will disappear in the twinkle of an eye. Commonsense dictates that you leave any valuables locked in the hotel safe, wear your camera around your neck, and use a money belt instead of a fat wallet in a back pocket. Report losses to the police

immediately. Though there is little chance of your property being recovered, a police report will assist with insurance claims.

Customs Regulations

Duty-free allowance on arrival in Jamaica are: 200 cigarettes or 25 cigars or 1lb of tobacco; 1 litre of wine and ½ litre of spirits (except rum). Restricted items include coffee, plants, flowers, fruit and vegetables. Imported currency which has a value over US$10,000 (about £6,000) must be declared.

Departure Tax

There is a J$500 departure tax payable at the airport when you leave.

Disabled People

The Jamaica Tourist Board has details of hotels with facilities for disabled visitors. These all feature ramps, adapted bathrooms and reserved parking spaces. Make careful enquiries before you book your hotel, as many have steep cliff paths or steps down to the beach. Hotels in Negril usually have better access as they tend to be built on a single level.

Driving

Jamaicans drive on the left. Simple speed restrictions are enforced with a 30mph (48kph) limit in town, and a 50mph (80kph) limit on the highway. Apart from in larger towns and the main road along the north coast, roads can be fairly basic, with few signs,

bone-shaking potholes, and tortuous twists and turns in hilly areas. Leave plenty of extra time for car journeys – you will get nowhere in a hurry. Car horns are a popular form of greeting, as well as warning, so do not take offence. People standing by the roadside waving their arms are not threatening, but asking for a lift. Fuel stations are generally open Monday to Saturday 07.30 to 19.00hrs; most are closed on Sunday and sometimes Wednesday. Do not expect to use a credit card.

Drugs

Marijuana (*ganja*) is a major Jamaican export crop, but it is also illegal. Dealers will approach you in the street or on the beach, and the drug is easily accessible. However, penalties are stiff, with a first-offence conviction for possession leading to a hefty fine and possible imprisonment or deportation.

Electricity

This is 110–220 volts, 50 cycles AC.

Embassies and Consulates

Australia: Australian High Commission, Kingston, (tel: 926 3550)
Canada: Canadian High Commission, 30 Knutsford Boulevard, Kingston 5 (tel: 926 1500)
UK: British High Commission, 26 Trafalgar Road, Kingston 10 (tel: 926 9050)
US: United States Embassy, 2 Oxford Road, Kingston 5 (tel: 929 4850)

DIRECTORY

Emergency Telephone Numbers

Ambulance and Fire
Department: 110
Police and Air-Sea Rescue: 119.

Entertainment Information

Events are well advertised in
Jamaica. Jamaica Tourist Board
offices in all the main centres
can provide information over
the counter, as can your hotel;
or consult the entertainments
section of the *The Daily Gleaner*,
which also publishes a monthly
guide.

Health

There are no vaccination
requirements for Jamaica, but it
is advisable to check with a
tropical disease unit, your airline
or travel agent in case any
precautions have been
recommended. They may
advise polio, tetanus, typhoid
and hepatitis vaccinations. Tap
water is drinkable and
standards of hygiene are
generally good. Mosquitoes can
be a real problem, so do not
stint on the insect repellent.
Birth-control is not a big issue in
Jamaica, and the use of
condoms limited, which has led
to an alarming incidence of
heterosexual AIDS. Government
hospitals in Kingston and
Mandeville provide medical
services at reasonable rates, but
it is always recommended to
take out full health insurance
before you leave home.
Jamaican sun is potent stuff, so
bring an adequate supply of
sunblock.

Holidays (Public and Religious)

New Year's Day
Ash Wednesday
Good Friday
Easter Monday
Labour Day: 23 May

Clarendon Plains

Independence Day: first
   Monday in August
National Hero's Day: third
   Monday in October
Christmas Day
Boxing Day

Marriage

You can get married 24 hours
after arriving in Jamaica, if you
have applied for your marriage
licence and submitted proof of
status. You will need proof of
citizenship (certified copy of
birth certificate, signed by a
public notary, which includes
father's name); parent's written
consent if under 21; proof of
divorce or being widowed, if
applicable.

Media

The best local paper is *The Daily
Gleaner. The Jamaica Herald* is
also a daily, and *The Star* an
evening tabloid. There are two
television stations, which dish

out a menu of US soaps; plus a
handful of local radio stations
with a greater preponderance of
phone-in chat shows than
reggae.

Money Matters

Foreign currency and travellers'
cheques can be cashed at
banks, *bureaux de change* or
your hotel. Banks offer the best
rates. The Jamaican dollar
divides into 100 cents. There
are 1, 5, 10, 20, 25, 50, J$1 and
J$5 coins, and 2, 5, 10, 20, 50,
100 and 500 dollar notes. In
tourist areas prices are often
quoted in US dollars, and US
currency is accepted legally in
hotels and illegally in numerous
stores. Purchases in duty-free
shops must be paid for in
foreign currency. Major credit
cards and travellers' cheques
are widely accepted in tourist-
orientated retail outlets, good
restaurants and hotels, but
check first and do not expect
fuel stations or smaller eating
places to take them. When
exchanging currency ask for
small denomination notes – it is
often difficult to get change.

Opening Times
Banks
Monday to Thursday 09.00 to
14.00hrs, Friday 09.00hrs to
noon and 14.30 to 17.00hrs.
Businesses
Normal business hours are
Monday to Friday 08.30 or 09.00
to 16.30 or 17.00hrs. Offices are
closed on weekends.
Shopping
Generally Monday to Friday
08.30 or 09.00 to 17.00hrs,

Saturday until 18.00hrs. In tourist areas there is usually plenty of opportunity for shopping on Sunday. Downtown Kingston has half-day closing on Wednesday, and stores in Uptown Kingston have half-day closing on Thursday.

Personal Safety

This is largely a matter of commonsense in Jamaica (see **Crime**, page 120). It is unwise to carry large amounts of cash or valuables, and foolish to enter the shantytown areas of West Kingston, such as Trench Town. Women travelling alone are likely to receive several good-natured propositions: a polite 'no thanks' will probably suffice.

Pharmacies

Pharmacies are plentiful in Jamaica, and most sell a wide range of goods, such as sweets and newspapers, beachballs and gifts, in addition to medicines and toiletries.

Places of Worship

Jamaica is commonly reputed to have more churches per square mile (or per person) than any other country in the world. Anglicans, Adventists, Baptists, Methodists and Roman Catholics will find churches throughout the island; Jamaica's only synagogue is in Kingston.

Police

The Jamaican police force is supposedly up to its collective neck in the island's drug problem, and there is little chance of recovering stolen goods. Otherwise, police are helpful with directions, and sympathetic when filling out theft reports. (In an emergency tel: 119.)

Postal Services

Jamaica is well supplied with post offices, but deliveries are slow and can take up to a week within the island itself. Overseas mail is likely to be equally slow. Post offices are open during normal business hours; there are no home deliveries, so all mail is addressed to and collected from post office box numbers.

Public Transport
Air

Trans Jamaica Airlines operate an internal flight service linking Kingston, Montego Bay, Negril, Ocho Rios and Port Antonio. Prices are reasonable and tickets can be booked direct or through a travel agent.

Bus and Minibus

Single-deck 'Coaster' buses (more comfortable) and minibuses are a cheap method of transport around the island, but services are unreliable and departures erratic at best. Drivers will not leave the bus station unless the vehicle is full, and by that they mean packed out. The Jamaica Tourist Board offices have schedules and fare information.

Taxis

Taxis are easily located at airports and hotels, or can be hailed in the street. They display red PPV (Public Passenger Vehicle) plates; some have an additional 'Tourism' plate which indicates that they have passed a more rigorous inspection.

Rates are regulated, but if a taxi is not metered, agree on a price before you set off. Hotels usually have a list of set fares, and suggested rates are displayed at airports. A 25 per cent surcharge is payable on rides between midnight and 05.00hrs; drivers also expect a tip.

Telephones

There are public telephones in most areas, but it is easier to make an international call than raise a number in the next town. Public telephones only take phone cards; they are available from telephone company offices and other authorised outlets, such as pharmacies and fuel stations. All overseas calls must go through the operator; any calls made from hotels will attract a hefty surcharge. To call Jamaica from the UK dial 001 809, followed by the subscriber's number.
Useful telephone numbers:
Directory assistance: dial 114
Local inter-island call operator: dial 112
International call operator: dial 113

Time

Jamaican time is the same as US Eastern Standard Time all year, which is five hours behind Greenwich Mean Time (and six hours behind UK time in spring and summer).

Tipping

Tipping is widely expected in Jamaica. Most hotels add a 10 to 12½ per cent service charge (apart from all-inclusive hotels where tips are already included); restaurants may add

Buses: cheap but unpredictable

around 10 to 15 per cent; but staff still expect a small gratuity. Although you pay upfront for a guided tour or raft trip, you should also tip your guide. Jamaicans expect photographers to ask permission before taking snaps of them, and a small tip.

Tourist Information

For information before you leave home, contact the Jamaica Tourist Board's overseas offices in:
Canada: 1 Eglinton Avenue East, Suite 616, Toronto M4P 3A1 (tel: 416-482 7850).
UK and Europe: 1–2 Prince Consort Road, London SW7 2BZ (tel: 0171-224 0505).
US: 801 Second Avenue, 20th Floor, New York, NY 10017 (tel: 212-856 9727).
The Tourist Board has local offices at:
2 St Lucia Avenue, Kingston 5 (tel: 929 9200).
Cornwall Beach, Montego Bay (tel: 952 4425).
Adrija Plaza, Negril (tel: 957 4243).
Ocean Village Shopping Centre, Ocho Rios (tel: 974 2570).
City Centre Plaza, Port Antonio (tel: 993 3051).
2 High Street, Black River (tel: 965 2074).

LANGUAGE

Jamaica is, of course, an English-speaking country. So you may be surprised to find that the language you commonly hear spoken is virtually incomprehensible. The colourful Jamaican patois has evolved from a wealth of different cultural influences over the centuries – its roots lie in 17th-century English, with a blend of regional British intonations (like Welsh and Scottish) and West African words, expressions, grammatical structure and pronunciation. More recently the Rastafarian dialect has crept into common speech; some of their words have 'I' substituted at the beginning, due to their emphasis on the importance of the individual. The following examples will give you a little taste of Jamaican patois – it includes some unfamiliar words plus a few phonetic spellings of (more-or-less) English words and phrases:

Babylon the established order (Church, State, the West), or figures of authority like the police

bangarang baggage

ben dung plaza stalls set out on the pavement (bend down plaza)

big gill a little more than ¼ pint (75ml)

bo-bo foolish person

boonoonoonoos delightful, the best

bredrin Rasta brothers

a chain not far (literally 22 yards)

cho man (mon) never mind, no problem

clot cloth

dat that

de gal dem the girls

de house dem the houses

dreadlocks Rasta locks of hair

duppy ghost

herb ('erb) ganja, marijuana

I an' I we

irie in harmony with the universe, just right, great

isire desire

ital pure, natural foods (vegetarian) or lifestyle

ivine divine

labrish discussion

likkle little

maga (maaga) thin woman

mash up (op) badly beaten, break, in turmoil

me wan fi go don ton I want to go downtown

mumpy fat woman

nyam to eat

one love Rasta greeting or parting expression

putta–putta mud

rass backside (either very rude or affectionate)

riddim rhythm

soon come sometime sooner or later, take your time

teet teeth

tenky thank you

walk good parting expression

wha fi do what to do

yea man (mon) yes (very commonly used for agreement, to men and women)

INDEX

INDEX/ACKNOWLEDGEMENTS

Acknowledgements

The Automobile Association wishes to thank the following photographers and libraries for their assistance in the preparation of this book.

AA PHOTO LIBRARY Roy Victor took all the photographs in this book with the exception of pages 55 and 63 which were taken by Jon Wyand

INTERNATIONAL PHOTOBANK Cover Ocho Rios, 53 Prospect Plantation

JAMES DAVIS TRAVEL PHOTOGRAPHY 34 Greenwood Great House, 66 Somerset Falls

MARY EVANS PICTURE LIBRARY 14 Rebellion

NATURE PHOTOGRAPHERS LTD 104 Pelican (P R Sterry), 107 Bananaquits (W S Paton)

SPECTRUM COLOUR LIBRARY 59 Port Antonio Harbour, 80 Limbo dancer, 83 Blue Mountain Peak

A WILSON 88 Spanish Town, 96 Treasure Beach

Copy editor for original edition: Dilys Jones
For this revision: Copy editor Colin Follett
Thanks also to Annie Wilson for all her revision work